HOW TO BE AN IMPORTER AND PAY FOR YOUR WORLD TRAVEL

HOW TO BE AN IMPORTER AND PAY FOR YOUR WORLD TRAVEL

MARY GREEN
STANLEY GILLMAR

TEN SPEED PRESS

To my husband, Steve Swig
and my children, Jocelyn and Samantha
Hail to the pie pies!
— Mary

to the women in my life
my mother, Ruth
my wife, Constance
my daughters, Sara, Amy, and Robin
— Stan

Ten Speed Press
P.O. Box 7123
Berkeley, California 94707

Book and cover design and typography by Fifth Street Design

First published by Celestial Arts in 1979

Library of Congress Cataloging in Publication Data

Green, Mary, 1942–
How to be an importer and pay for your world travel. / Mary Green, Stanley Gillmar. — Rev.
p. cm.
ISBN 0-89815-501-0 $8.95
1. Commerce. 2. Self-employment. I. Gillmar, Stanley, 1935- II. Title.
HF1007.G678 1993
658.8—dc20 92-34113
CIP

Printed in the United States of America
3 4 5 — 97 96 95

TABLE OF CONTENTS

Chapter 1

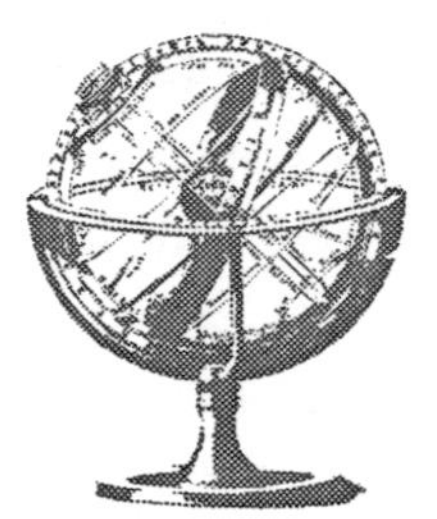

THE IMPORTING GAME

Several years ago on a trip to North Africa, we found some striking, hand-painted silk scarves in a small shop in the bazaar. The designs were sophisticated and the colors were unusual. We purchased a number of them hoping others would like them as well. Since then those scarves have sold in some of the finest shops in San Francisco. We were able to reorder again and again and ultimately we made thousands of dollars, more than enough to offset the cost of our vacation. That's the Importing Game!

The festive hair ornaments worn by peasant women in one remote area of the world were so bright and beautiful they reminded us of Christmas. We bought and sold them as Christmas ornaments. That was the initial step in what developed into a delightful Importing Game experience, as we added small toys and traditional craftwork of all sorts from many different countries. The bright colors, unusual textures and unique designs have added a new and interesting concept to Christmas decorations.

On a trip to Afghanistan, we discovered the traditional and distinctive hand-knitted socks of that area. We have sold hundreds of dozens of them since and recovered far in excess of our travel expenses through the Importing Game.

What is the Importing Game? It is simply purchasing goods which can be sold in the United States for a profit while traveling abroad (for business and pleasure).

Well, of course! you say. That's simple. The problem is, what do you buy? How do you buy it? What about paying duties? Clearing customs? Where do you sell it after you get it back? Actually, you'll find these seemingly complex problems aren't as insurmountable as you think. It's really not complicated; it can be fun, and you can make money.

Think for a moment about your last trip to Europe, Canada or other foreign country. Did you bring something back that you bought there? Did you show your purchase to any of your friends? Did they admire it? Did they say they wished they had one? Weren't you an importer who had just discovered a market?

You bought an article that appealed to you. And, since the things you like are often things your friends like, you bought something which could be sold. It was probably less expensive in the country of its origin than something comparable here would be. Possibly, it was uncommon or even unobtainable here. In either case, it seemed worth buying and bringing back. So, it is quite possible it might sell here at a price somewhat higher than what it cost you to buy it and bring it back home.

So you see, what you liked other people liked also. You probably could have sold it (had you not wanted it yourself) for more than it cost you. Had you done so, you would have imported goods which you had chosen and sold them at a profit. That's the Importing Game. It's just that easy.

On a trip to London one year we bought an unusual and well-produced book on wines. Many of our friends who were interested in wines, when they saw our book, wished to own a copy for themselves. Some asked where we bought ours and offered to buy it. We didn't sell our copy, of course, and they couldn't obtain other copies in the U.S. Ultimately, an American edition was produced and distributed at a price considerably higher than we had paid. If we had been aware of the Importing Game at that time, we could have sold the book for twice what we had paid. At the same time we would have made our friends happy because they would gladly have paid that amount for the book.

Not everything from abroad will sell well, of course. Tourist knickknacks are certainly not likely to sell to people other than those traveling in the country to which these items relate, although we've even found an exception to that rule. We've brought back T-shirts from Tahiti and other exotic places. All sorts of people wanted the Hinano beer T-shirt with the label showing the winsome tropical lass. The shirt with the flower-like logo of Air Polynesia was also popular. In fact, T-shirts are so popular everywhere that you could easily start a two-way trade in them. On our most recent trip to Spain, a young woman we met was particularly proud of her T-shirt—from U.C.L.A.!

Of course, it would be extremely unwise to start out too big and too fast. You do it in stages until you get the feel of it. Obviously, you wouldn't buy five hundred T-shirts on the chance you could sell them. That is too large a capital outlay and much too risky. Buy a dozen of so of a particular kind or a representative variety. That is how we approached our initial silk scarf purchase; they were well received so we purchased more. However, had they not been an immediate success, we still would have made several hundred dollars on the initial purchase and been ahead of the Game. If it is possible to make advance arrangements to order more if the response proves favorable, so much the better. If not, you learn about your taste and people's reactions to it. On your next trip you have more confidence in your ability to purchase what people will buy. Hopefully, you will have also increased your purchasing capital. You can take more of a risk; put more into your buying program.

Sometimes you will get such a positive response to your purchases that it will justify a return trip for additional stock and possibly renegotiation for larger quantities. We had anticipated that the Afghan socks would become popular and had arranged for further shipments if our initial sales indicated a sufficient demand. However, the volume of orders was so great that it necessitated a trip back to Kabul to assure that the arrangements were workable with the increased shipments and that our customers' delivery dates would be met.

Certain products are of limited availability or require your personal selection—those you have to buy right then and there, and it is often difficult to decide how much to buy. The more confidence you have in your ability to judge the market, the more you will buy and be tempted to buy.

The fact that you have come this far is a demonstration of your interest in playing the Importing Game. But first you need to know the basic rules, and, to make it fun, some advice on how to win. Let's start with the fun part. The first and best advice is—"buy what you like." That may sound too simple at first, but think about it. You know about the things that already interest you. You are certainly more sensitive to them than you are to items which hold no special allure for you. You're more aware of the quality, the selection, the price.

A friend of ours buys old grandfather clocks on trips to England, has them shipped home, and sells them to decorators. Sometimes she has six or eight grandfather clocks in various rooms of her home until they are sold. She is a successful participant in the Importing Game. On the other hand, it wouldn't work for us to import clocks of that sort. They aren't of particular interest to us. We don't own one, don't really have a desire to own one and so have little sensitivity toward design, quality or the market for them. We would probably make some bad purchasing decisions and be unable to sell them.

That brings up another good reason for buying what you like. The first is that you will do a better job of purchasing. The second is that you won't mind keeping the items if they don't prove marketable. Let's face it, even the best professional buyers goof on occasion. One of the reasons stores have clearance sales is to get rid of some of those errors. But if you like what you've bought, you're going to enjoy having it yourself if it doesn't sell. You can use those interesting African textiles for tablecloths, pillows, wall hangings and even for unique clothes. You will also be proud to give them as gifts. After all, if you've chosen well they will be highly appreciated by friends and relatives as gifts you brought from your trip. So those duplicates you can't use yourself will turn out to be excellent solutions to future gift problems. Some of those North African scarves which had been shown as samples were later highly treasured by friends.

The market for any product consists of those people who like it and want to have it. It is a group of people who react to what you bought just the way you did. How do you find these potential customers?

Initially, you probably need look no further than home. We all tend to associate with a number of people who have interests and tastes similar to our own. So show your purchases to your friends and acquaintances.

We brought back a group of unusual batiks from Indonesia one year. We had acquired these because they were more sophisticated and, we felt, more desirable, despite their somewhat higher cost, than the selection of Indonesian batiks normally found in the U.S. The enthusiastic response and fascination of some of our friends suggested significant potential. They wanted to buy our samples. The positive reaction of our friends was indicative of market interest, which was subsequently confirmed by sales to boutiques.

So, your friends provide an easily approached test market and a likely group of initial customers. We bought one beautifully ornate, antique Afghan coat for personal use on our first buying trip to that country. We could have sold dozens. We finally decided to order more for a few friends who were close to us, but distant from each other. We limited our sales in order to maintain their distinctiveness. Those friends are, of course, happy with that decision. They each bought a beautiful coat at a good price, and are not likely to see duplicates.

And that, of course is the reason why the Importing Game is so enjoyable. You get to travel to unique and fascinating places and often get more intimately involved with the customs and cultures of those societies. You become acquainted with the shopkeepers, their employees, and possibly suppliers, and others who don't often see or do business with tourists.

In addition to having attractive imports for your own daily use and pleasure, you often make friends and acquaintances happy by making available to them unique and beautiful merchandise which they wouldn't be able to find, or would only find at a much higher price.

There is also the opportunity to make money, sometimes in substantial amounts, while doing many of the things you would do anyway on a trip. You simply buy more items, with a slightly different emphasis, keep what you want, and sell the excess. The seller benefits, you benefit, and the buyers benefit.

Wouldn't you like to play a game where everybody wins?

Chapter 2

WHAT TO BUY

While traveling during the past several years, we discovered many beautiful and interesting articles which struck us as potential purchases for resale. Some we liked immediately and purchased without a second thought. Others required more evaluation. Some sold quickly, some took more time. Others, which never sold at all, became Aunt Helen's birthday presents. What was the difference? How do you decide what to buy? What has the best potential to sell at a profit?

To successfully play the Importing Game you need to do a little planning. Of course, many successful purchases are items you would never have considered until you saw them. However, that can be risky unless you have a fairly good sense of the market for those particular goods. Generally, it is a good idea to think about the things you might like to sell and where you might want to go to get them.

We try to follow four basic rules. These guidelines do not assure success, but they help to keep your goal in mind while making purchases in romantic places, where buying on impulse is a common occurrence. They are: 1) buy what you like, 2) buy within your own specialty, 3) buy what you won't mind reselling, and 4) don't be afraid to buy!

≈ BUY WHAT YOU LIKE ≈

"Buy what you like" sounds simple. It is a basic rule of the Importing Game and is as simple as it sounds. You will feel more confident about purchasing and about the article's subsequent appeal to others. By purchasing items that you personally like, you begin the Game with an advantage. Because you probably will have some prior knowledge about those items which you enjoyed purchasing and owning in the past, you are on familiar ground and ahead of others.

Having made purchases in the past of items you liked, you have been involved in the market for these goods; you are, in fact, a determining force in that market. You have selected certain types of items over others—perhaps even similar ones. You already have a working knowledge of the market supply of these goods, price variations, and differences in quality. Some have generated more comments from your friends and acquaintances than others.

Think about comments of your friends and others who have been exposed to your purchases in the past. In this way you develop your own personal market survey. After all, they, and people like them, will determine the ultimate market for goods you want to sell.

Some of our more spectacular adventures in buying items we didn't really feel comfortable with (or like at all) occurred during our earlier expeditions, when we were concentrating on the Middle East rather than Europe. Because of the bargaining culture of the Middle East and because we kept running into items we had not seen before, we often found ourselves caught up in the excitement of the marketplace and the people. We bargained for items we didn't even want, not realizing until later that we had wasted our time and energy and spent part of our "importing budget" unwisely.

While buying what you like seems a simple and logical game plan, there are some important qualifications. A distressing example which violated several of those qualifications occurred in the Middle East. We loved lapis lazuli jewelry—being drawn to that wonderful blue. But we knew nothing about its quality differences or its sales potential. Somehow, however, while taking tea in a shop and discussing lapis generally, we found ourselves purchasing more than one hundred dollars' worth of cheap lapis and white metal jewelry. It started with purchasing one which Mary liked very much and somehow, without realizing it, purchasing more because we thought they might sell—even though we didn't particularly like them. We were purchasing something we liked (lapis) but set in a design we did not like at all. We became sidetracked and were concentrating on only one part of the item—the part we liked!

The example also illustrates another difficulty which can arise when you begin to purchase items for resale. That is trying to "second-guess" the market, i.e., purchasing items you don't really care for because you think someone else might. Beginning the Game with "second-guessing" usually results in buying mistakes. If you don't particularly like those goods, you usually don't know what people who do like them are actually looking for. The lapis lazuli jewelry is a good example of our trying to anticipate what others might like. We loved the lapis stone, but knew little about its quality differences or its market. We were really basing our purchases on the fact that we like lapis color and had heard that "lapis sells."

Additionally, in this instance, not only were we caught up in the excitement of a new market, but we ran into a recurrent hazard—the smooth seller. We allowed ourselves to be led astray by a fast-talking merchant who convinced us that the prices for this jewelry were exceptionally low. He also convinced us that the design, combined with these unusually low prices, would have potential buyers beating down our doors.

No one beat our doors down. We had allowed ourselves to put aside our own judgment on design, desirability and cost, and be guided by someone who simply wanted to make a sale and was well trained at doing so. The jewelry did eventually sell; however, it was much, much later, and then for not more than we had paid. We realized no return on our investment, let alone profit for all our trouble.

On several other occasions, in various parts of the Middle East, we were sidetracked by smooth operators and purchased things we liked without considering whether they were suitable for resale. Once we added two camel bags to our growing number of purchases and another time, thirty-five totally useless, gold embroidered hats, just because the man was so charming and we got caught up in the place and the people and forgot we were spending real money! This is another common pitfall. When you are spending foreign money, sometimes you don't realize how much you are actually spending—it almost seems like "play money." Keep track of it carefully!

While traveling it often seems that you "like" everything. Things are unusual and carry with them the "romance" of the place you are visiting. Some of our "giveaways" were purchased under just such conditions. So keep in mind that there is value in hesitating before making the decision to purchase for resale. It is wise to prepare a short checklist for yourself, mental or actual. Just before saying yes, ask:

1. Is this really what I want? Unique? Attractive? Good quality?
2. Will it really sell or am I kidding myself?
3. Is the price one that will allow me the markup I need to sell it at a profit?
4. Will there be problems in getting it home? Bulk? Breakage?
5. Can I anticipate any unusual problems with this commodity? Food or drug? Quotas?
6. What about reorders?

Just think a bit about it and you can add you own questions.

In Afghanistan we discovered some traditional embroidered leather footwear which we liked immediately—perfect, we felt, for after-ski and the rapidly approaching Christmas season. We purchased two hundred pair without a second thought. There were, unfortunately, a number of attendant problems directly related to their resale value. We could have foreseen the most serious of these difficulties had we spent a bit more time thinking about this purchase.

First of all, the boots smelled heavily of leather and the curing process of the area added seriously to that smell. This presented problems in shipping them with something else which might (and in our case did!) pick up the smell. It also raised the serious question of whether anyone over here would purchase them.

Secondly, the boots were in fact very seasonal and very ethnic looking. Their leather, fur and brightly colored red and green embroidered designs made them look particularly like Christmas items. We were purchasing them close to Christmas so there was a very real problem of timing. Could we get two hundred pairs of them back to the United States in time to sell them for Christmas? We could not hand-carry them because they weighed too much. An alternate and more costly shipping arrangement was necessary.

We later learned that most stores purchase for their Christmas market many months in advance and are unable to commit to new merchandise so close to Christmas. We did not know this at that time, and so wouldn't have considered it. We filed it away for future reference and we pass the information on to you. Most stores commit for items months ahead of the time they actually plan to merchandise them. Of course, some also keep money aside for the wonderful new and unusual items which they will come across in the months after major commitments have been made. But they are usually prepared to purchase for winter in spring and spring in winter, so you are not foreclosed most times of the year. Large quantities of seasonal goods are harder to sell as the selling season approaches because the buyer's money is oftentimes tied up in inventory which must be sold before other purchases can be made.

So we had to wait to sell our boots. Eventually we did recover a substantial portion of our trip costs. But, if we had spent a day thinking it over, we probably would have purchased not two hundred pairs of boots but perhaps a dozen or so as a test, packaged them separately from the clothing in our suitcases and hand-carried them back in time for the Christmas sales period. We'd have reduced our substantial freight costs and the year's delay. Also, had the initial dozen or so proven very popular, this would have allowed us to make arrangements to presell a large order for the next Christmas season with little or no risk.

The situation with the boots exemplifies several problems which we could have foreseen. We liked them the first time we saw them—but we should have questioned the number and our motives. Did they remind us of Afghanistan and did we simply want to retain that memory—or was their design attractive and desirable? Keep in mind you might like something because it reminds you of a particular place. But is it fine enough to consider for resale? You should questions *why* you like it.

You might like something because it reminds you of a past lover, prior trip, or your personal predilection for anything with red in it, good or bad. This could affect your buying. You want to buy things that you like for their quality, design, and other salable attributes, not for the memories they hold for you. We all have some things which we buy and keep and like because they remind us of something our mother or favorite relative owned—but other than that we would not purchase them. Also, you do not personally have to want to "own" everything that you buy. You can admire an item, like it for its good qualities and feel confident that others will like it. We all can remember seeing things in friends' homes or articles of clothing that others have worn which we have admired for the design but would not have wanted to own ourselves.

To illustrate this point, while traveling in Spain we discovered some outstanding cinch belts with handsome metal buckles. We purchased about a dozen as samples after considerable discussion with the designer about their sales potential. (Keep in mind that what you are told sells over there may relate to entirely different markets and may *not* sell over here.) In this instance Mary had bought what she liked and would want to wear, as well as what she liked but would not have personally worn. However, we were persuaded by the seller to purchase some that were "good sellers" over there, even though we did not like them. We felt confident about our choices because we felt we knew the particular and rather specialized market of women's accessories and the general high quality of design was impressive. The belts we picked out sold well. The others (the ones that "sold well" in Spain but that we were doubtful about) did not sell. American women seem to have a different feeling for design than women in Spain or the tourists from Scandinavia who abound in the Costa del Sol and buy these belts there. We felt that ours sold because we were purchasing those which we genuinely liked for their design whether we wanted to wear them or not. This was a product with which we were familiar and with which we felt comfortable.

Another pitfall is the purchase of something that is "not quite right" with the intention of changing it just a little to perfect it and insure its salability. Do this only if you are sure you actually have the time to make the necessary changes, and be realistic about its salability once the changes are made. We have made this error, particularly with clothing. Actually we didn't like what we were buying, but thought that by changing it we would like it. By altering it (if we ever got around to it!) the interesting aspect of it was changed too, and we liked it even less.

The imports which sell best are those which cannot be easily duplicated in the United States; these are items that are unusual and have a great appeal for just that reason. Naturally, items which can be made easily in the United States carry a lower price tag over here. On one occasion we discovered some lovely handbags in Europe which we attempted to sell in the

United States. They were outstandingly beautiful but not unusual enough as an import. Their necessarily high price tag did not allow them to compete with similar handbags of the same high quality and design made in the United States which had a significantly lower pricing structure.

Finally, do not fall into the trap of wanting to purchase something simply for the sake of not coming home empty handed. More often than not this will cause you to end up purchasing something you do not really like or want or purchasing at too high a cost! Remember your budget! Keep in mind the lady who, before her world trips, would go to one of the import stores in town and buy souvenirs with labels "made in Mexico" or whatever country she was planning to visit. She had found they were generally just as inexpensive plus she saved herself the hassles of carrying them or shipping them. That's fine for the obligatory gifts. For resale items, they have to be unusual and attractive. Otherwise, just save your money.

≈ SPECIALIZE ≈

When we began to buy for resale, we found ourselves confused about what to choose from the many available, beautiful articles. We found jewelry, clothing, artifacts, and antiques everywhere, all exciting and waiting for someone to take them home. You cannot buy everything you like! Ultimately, after some unsuccessful purchases of items about which we had insufficient information or knowledge, we decided to change our approach. We made up our minds we would only buy things about which we had acquired some expertise prior to our trip.

Everyone has at least one area of interest that is "special" to them—in which they have knowledge through ancestral heritage, for which they have a natural affinity, or which they have studied, either formally or developed through personal curiosity. We have all been told at one time or another that we have a "natural" gift for something and chances are that each of us has spent time developing our natural talents or interests. But how do you locate those "special interests" among the confusion of all the possibilities? You will find that among all the things you own and like, you own more of a variety of some than of others. Perhaps it is music boxes, chessmen of unusual design or material, or handbags. You probably have more of those because of some special personal enjoyment.

As part of that enjoyment, you have most likely learned quite a bit about that group of items, having spent more time in the marketplace looking them over. You therefore have a specialty. No one is an expert in everything and specializing directs your energies into one area. Instead of trying to become an expert in the field of antique jewelry, women's clothing, rare stamps, clocks and old rifles, choose one—one in which you already have a working knowledge and upon which you can build. It is easier and safer. And, in the end you will be dealing with more compatible types of items and buyers.

To illustrate, Mary through the years had always been told she exhibited a "natural talent" for putting together color, texture and style to create attractive outfits for women. This was a talent which had already been developing and, therefore, we needed only to direct some energy and money into purchases which dealt with women's fashion. Her choices drew on a talent to foresee trends which she had been developing in personal life for many years.

Stan, on the other hand, had pursued an early interest in oriental artifacts and contemporary art, building his knowledge through reading, shopping and other methods of comparison wherever such artifacts were displayed. As a result he had developed a fair talent for finding interesting designs and evaluating prices, authenticity, and rarity of such items. This was, therefore, another possible area of specialization purchasing.

Purchasing in the areas of either a developed interest or a "natural talent" remarkably improved our buying skills. We made fewer mistakes and it required less time to make a decision. We didn't waste as much time looking at things that were of inferior quality. We found we had enough basic information so we did not waste valuable time attempting to obtain information necessary to make an intelligent decision at the moment of purchase. There was less chance for error in judgment because we had some bacground information already on costs, design difference, and other factors affecting a wise purchase for resale. And, we were less able to be led astray by a smooth seller.

So we found ourselves naturally "specializing," that is to say, we were devoting our efforts to a particular type of merchandise. We also found that by concentrating on a specialty, our sales effort when we returned was much reduced. We developed a reputation for outstanding items of a particular type and buyers seeking objects within our specialty began to call us. It became less and less necessary for us to make a concentrated sales effort after each trip. As we became more familiar with the tastes of customers, we actually purchased with some of them in mind—not knowing for certain that they would purchase the items, but feeling they probably would. In the end someone did and more often than not it was the person we had in mind.

In selling your goods to stores you find yourself dealing with the same people—developing a good relationship and a reputation for quality merchandise of a certain type. It is not necessary to chase around to ten or twenty stores after each trip in order to locate the one or two which handle the items you have purchased. With larger stores there are buyers for specific types of items, so rather than seeing ten different people, you are able to develop a relationship with the one or two who buy items in your specialty.

Additionally, by specializing you will gain knowledge of problems which may surround the purchase and resale of certain items. To illustrate, someone acquainted with antique guns will know that you are unable to bring firearms into the United States unless you have a specific type of permit. Your knowledge within your specialty will assist you in circumventing problems which may have prevented others from importing such items, and therefore make the merchandise even more valuable for resale.

We have a friend who has made substantial sums of money pursuing and investing in his specialty, vintage Mercedes automobiles. He knows their value and enjoys a developed natural talent for automotive repairs. He finds the cars in Europe in various states of disrepair. The search and circumstance is usually an adventure in itself. He purchases them, ships them back to the United States, repairs them, and resells them for a profit. He's making money and he's also enjoying himself! He chose this specialization from several possible ones because he enjoys it so much more than the others. He is directing all his energies into one area; he feels comfortable in it, deals with similarly interested sellers and buyers and automotive parts dealers. Because he is well acquainted with his specialty, he knows about the problems of licensing, of compliance with various environmental and safety standards, and other important details. Obviously the casual or one shot importer of such an item would be asking for trouble more often that not. With each purchase our friend is learning more about his market—as well as building his future trip fund.

Research can help you in developing a desired specialty or assist by making you more expert in an already existing specialty. By researching your market you can minimize problems related to purchasing. Through comparison shopping for example, you will gain insight and a wealth of information pertaining to quality differences, availability, pricing, and varieties of design. We will discuss in more detail some pleasant ways to conduct this research in Chapter 4.

≈ THE COLLECTOR PITFALL! ≈

Be sure to choose a specialty which encompasses items you will not mind reselling. In looking at our own "collections," we found that we loved primitive handicrafts of all types. Indeed, we had a marvelous collection we lived with, loved, and were continually increasing. We felt that because of our interest, taste and knowledge in this "specialized area" it would be a perfect type of item to buy and resell for profit. Unfortunately when we tried to buy some for resale we found it difficult to part with any of them. We had become too personally attached and did not really want to sell them. We kept saying we'd sell the next one. On one occasion we purchased two handmade birdcages in Tunisia for ten dollars apiece, confident we could make a good profit. We were offered two hundred dollars for them, but ultimately decided not to sell—even though we had two! We simply could not bear to part with either of them.

On a similar occasion we purchased two outstanding peasant rugs from a remote section of the Middle East for a hundred and forty dollars. We found that similar rugs sold for nine hundred dollars in the United States and we were offered substantial sums for ours. Even so, we could not bear to part with them. For purposes of the Importing Game, our money would have been better invested in other items. We were beginning to augment our handicraft collection at a much faster rate than we intended because we were not reselling our purchases. We were becoming collectors, not importers! There is a vast difference. Importers buy things with the specific intention of reselling them whether they would like to own these things or not. Collectors buy things because they are very interested in obtaining more of that particular class of articles for themselves.

We have one very good friend who started importing about fifteen years ago. He acquired some of the finest embroidered wall hangings in the world from certain remote areas. He would sell off a few at a time, very reluctantly, just enough to live on, but found it hard to part with the rest. He was becoming "attached." He stated that his ultimate goal was to develop a collection which would be auctioned off in New York sometime in the future. He is still "collecting" embroideries and we suspect that he will never have that auction. Yet, the same friend was one of the first to bring in the Turkish puzzle ring many years ago. He made substantial profits. For him, Turkish puzzle rings were much easier to part with than gorgeous wall hangings.

≈ DON'T BE AFRAID TO BUY ≈

What if it doesn't sell? What if no one wants it? These are all questions that you may ask yourself just prior to making a purchase. Review your checklist to be certain you are not being carried away by the excitement and mood of the moment. On the other hand, don't let fear set in or you'll never buy a thing. You have to begin somewhere, so begin the Game now! What if you do make a mistake and can't sell the item as quickly or for the price that you wish? One of the reasons we suggest that you begin by purchasing things you like is that in case it doesn't sell, you will not mind owning it, or giving it away as a tasteful gift. Realistically, you can generally sell anything purchased with taste for at least what your costs were, so you will probably not be out any money. Chapter 9 gives many pointers on this.

So take that plunge and start the Game now!

And now you're off, but where to?

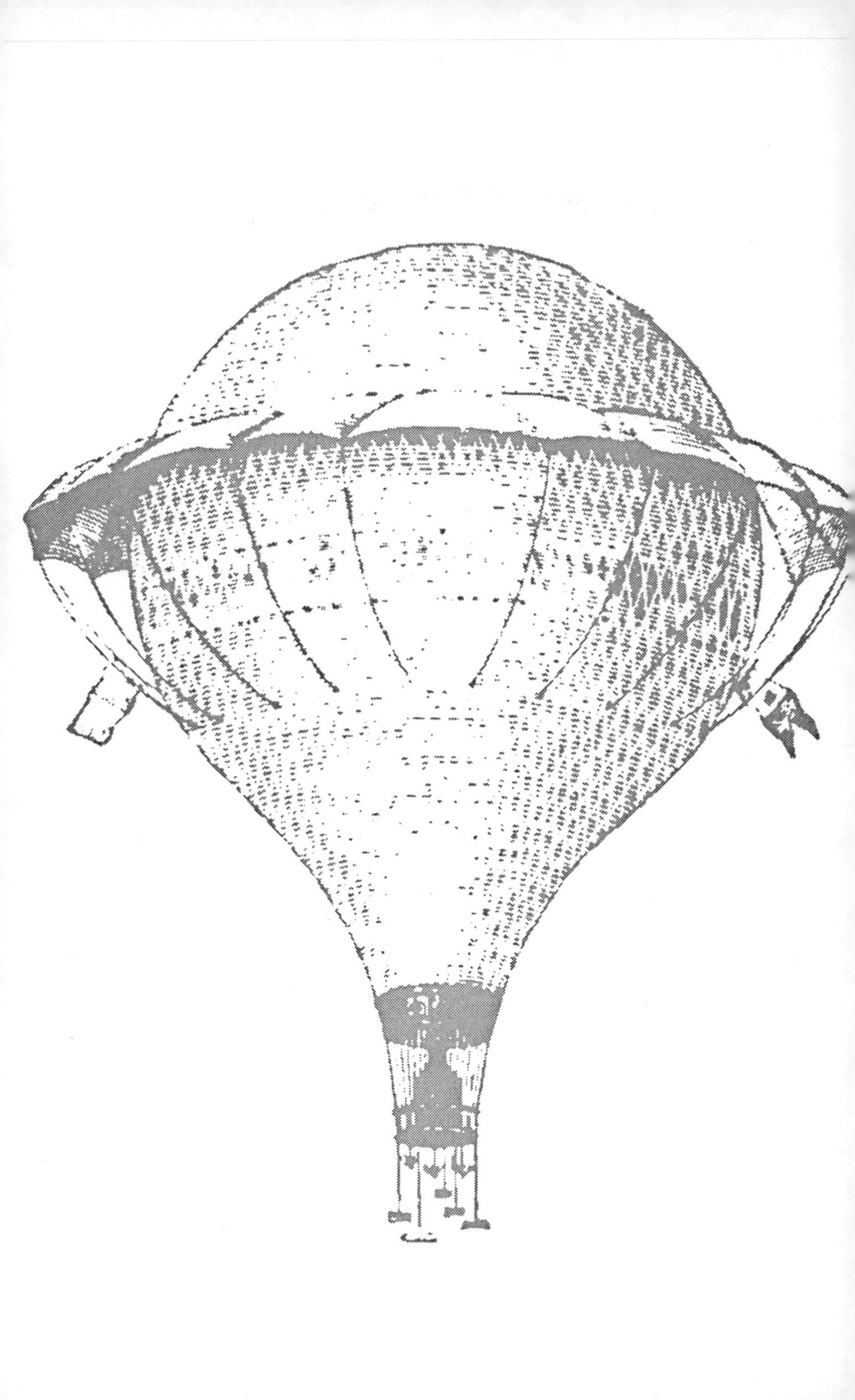

Chapter 3

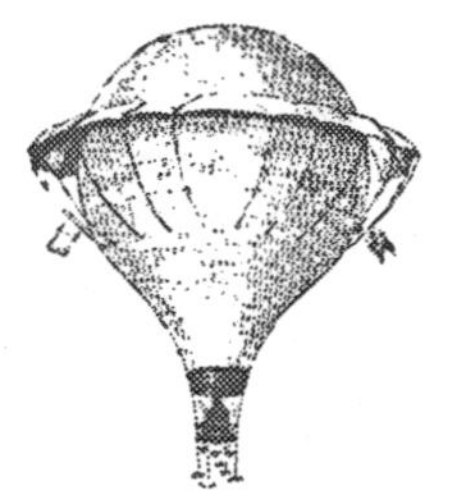

WHERE DO YOU GO? THAT'S EASY!

Now that you know a few basic rules and some of the general exceptions, how can you use that knowledge in planning where to go? Once you've decided the kinds of objects you want to purchase on your trip, you probably have narrowed down your choices considerably. If you want to buy brightly colored textiles of Central America, you probably would want to start in Guatemala, since that is the most accessible point in Central America other than Panama, and many of the markets have outstanding displays.

Let's take another example. Say you wanted to import some of those wonderful carved tribal utensils from the Somali Republic. After some preliminary inquiries, you might decide to start in Kenya rather than go to the Somali Republic capital, Mogadiscio. A closer look at why you might choose Nairobi as a base of operations will point out some of the factors involved in selecting a destination for your buying trip.

1. *Ease of Access* Between Cairo and Johannesburg, international flights destined for Africa's east side most frequently land in Nairobi. In less developed parts of the world frequency

of flights is as important as is the diversity of international air carriers.

Airlines in developing regions are often owned or controlled by their governments and thus must respond to demands other than service to their passengers. It is not unusual to find that the week's single flight out of a remote area will be inexplicably canceled or will overfly that airfield. Reservations may be lost or not honored. One may even be removed from a flight to make room for a local dignitary.

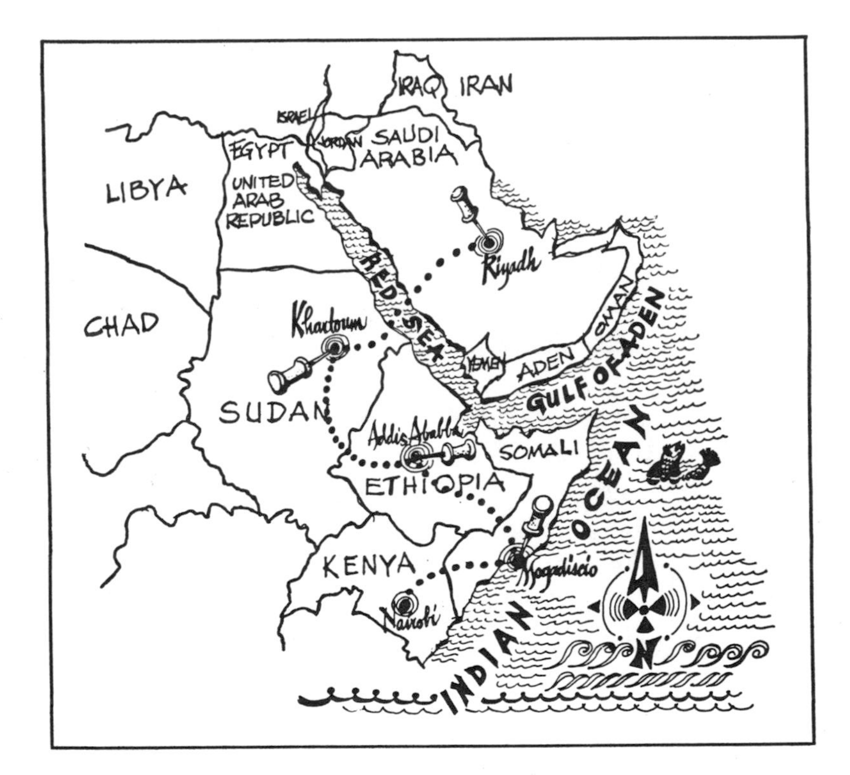

Ease of access involves not only the ease of your getting to and from your chosen base of operations, but also the ease of getting the product to a point from which it can be shipped home. For example, some of the goods we seek are made by tribes in the southern part of the Somali Republic and the southern part of the Sudan. Each of these are large countries and their southern borders are closer to Nairobi, Kenya, than to their own capitals. So, presuming there are no trade restraints at the border, Nairobi is a better base than any other.

2. *Cooperativeness* Does the country want you? Are the local officials predisposed to be of assistance? Will the people be helpful? The more disposed the particular country is to visitors and trade, the more likely you will find a cooperative attitude. In planning your hypothetical trip you become aware that at present there are problems in visiting Ethiopia and the Somali Republic. Kenya, on the other hand, is encouraging visitors, so, again Nairobi seems the better choice.

3. *Rules and Regulations* If, for example, you wanted to purchase ivory artifacts, you would have difficulty in Kenya, as there is a prohibition on ivory exports to help preserve the elephants. Otherwise, Kenya is probably the most commercial economy of those you are considering and probably has fewer restrictions on exports from the country. You can make a more detailed check of such restrictions by writing the embassy of each country and asking about export restrictions and regulations. However, these can be changed at any time, and, in developing countries or those experiencing political unrest, perhaps invented by the export inspector on the spot. Rely as much on the general attitudes in and reputation of the country as on the written regulations provided by their embassy.

4. *The Language* If you know the language, you are leagues ahead in finding the exact product you want and in bargaining for it; of course, in many parts of the world, particularly where you will uncover the most interesting potential imports, English is less likely to be common, and the native language less likely to be known by those who speak English. Kenya's English heritage again points to Nairobi as the best choice.

5. *Where do you want to go?* Last, but not least, is the question, what would you prefer? After all, this is the Importing Game. If you don't enjoy it, then it's no longer a game. If

you've always wanted to go to Kenya, if you would enjoy the high savannah area and the chance to see some game parks on the side, perhaps Nairobi is the best choice for you. On the other hand, you might be intrigued by the unique history and culture of Ethiopia and choose Addis Ababa or want to explore the Arab influences in the seacoast town of Mogadiscio in the Somali Republic. However, recently both of these areas have been troubled with political unrest and would not be practical alternatives.

Thus, for many reasons, you would probably choose Nairobi today for a base of operations to buy tribal artifacts from the border tribes in the nations along and across the northern border of Kenya.

The simple rule implicit in the foregoing example is to buy items at the place where they are made, or as reasonably close to it as practicable. The rule seems so basic you almost feel it is self-evident, and yet, many violate it—sometimes without thinking and sometimes because of a lack of knowledge.

For instance, we once brought a striking antelope carving in Kenya. It seemed somewhat higher in price than other carvings we had seen there, but its design was so strong and it was so unlike anything else we had seen that we bought it. That purchase got us interested in African art and we soon discovered that the piece was West African rather than from a tribe in Kenya. That's why the piece was unlike anything else we saw and why its price was higher. In contrast, some of the carved items of everyday utility—bells, spoons, bowls—which were characteristic of the woodworking of East Africa were purchases of outstanding quality and value.

You want to buy things where they're made, or as close as you can get. That requires you to find out where things are made. If you are traveling and come across something you like but that you don't know much about, try to find out more. Ask questions and try to establish precisely where the articles were made.

On a trip to Indonesia, we found many attractive batiks in Bali. Some were old or antique and others were new. Discussions with shopkeepers confirmed that most of the new batiks were produced in Jogjakarta. We purchased only older batiks in Bali and deferred our purchases of new material till we reached "Jogja." We were rewarded by a much greater selection of traditional designs and some unusual special designs (such as the cloud band pattern), which were not considered popular and so were not generally distributed to other places in Indonesia.

Having found where items are made, you decide what you want to buy and then go to that place for your purchases. We enjoy rough glazed Japanese pottery, but find it almost impossible to obtain it in the U.S. On a trip to Japan we saw some pieces in Tokyo shops specializing in materials for the tea ceremony. The pieces were outstanding, but so were the prices. We waited, since we knew that the traditional source of that type of pottery was in southern Japan. Ultimately, in Kurashiki, near the area where they are produced, we found several shops with an excellent selection of the modern Bizenware that we wanted. And the prices were much more reasonable.

So the basic rule is to buy where things are—or were—made. Like all rules, this one, too, has exceptions. A friend of ours who is a dealer in oriental rugs was leaving on a trip to Iran and Afghanistan. We were enthusiastic about joining him on his trip with the hope of acquiring some rugs at good prices. While desiring our company, he suggested that we not go with the intention of finding any rugs. The prices of older rugs, which is what we would be seeking, had increased so greatly, particularly in Iran, that they were actually cheaper in the U.S.

When a country with strong cultural identity achieves affluence in the world, its people often begin to buy works of art of their own culture. Since they usually know more about their own art than anyone else, and are relatively more interested in it, the prices within that society rise. During that time, prices for older things will be more expensive in the country of origin than elsewhere. A few years ago, a friend of ours who sells Japanese antiques noted that the bulk of his buyers were Japanese visiting the U.S. They found the prices here so much cheaper than in Japan that they were buying Japanese antiques in the U.S. and shipping them back to Japan.

Another exception which relates to older things has to do with old trade routes and patterns of movement of people and goods. Some of our best buys in Chinese trade porcelains of the Sung period were found in Indonesia and the Philippines, since these islands were part of the old trade routes of the Chinese. Knowing that the Moors of North Africa at one time occupied southern Spain and Portugal will explain some of the motifs you find there and, if you are sensitive to Arabic art forms, may enable you to find articles there which are bypassed by other buyers. In other words, keep your eyes open for your specialty items in unexpected places. You would not expect to find an English antique in a small shop in Southeast Asia. But when you do, you will probably know more about it than does the shopkeeper.

Two of the best Persian rugs we have were acquired at ridiculously low prices a few years ago, in, of all places, Hawaii. Why? Because some of the people who settled there originally came from England and New England, where oriental rugs have been enjoyed for decades. But wool rugs are inappropriate in the tropics and after a generation or two, none of the family knew why those old rugs ought to be saved. Similarly, none of the shopkeepers had much experience with them so they were for sale at very low prices.

Another exception to the rule applies, particularly in certain developing countries. If you go to the source of the objects you may find the quality is not as good, the prices are not lower, and that you will have difficulty getting the items out of these sometimes remote areas. Often, the best goods are shipped to the large cities for resale. The merchants who purchase in the hinterlands select the finer quality stock and the lesser quality items are rejected. As the markup from maker to merchant to ultimate retail customer on items in these countries is often only about twenty percent (not our usual hundred percent) you are not saving much by going to the source.

Additionally, getting bulky items out of a remote area is often costly and occasionally impossible. Of the several styles of gloves we bought in Afghanistan, one came from a very remote and inaccessible area in the middle of the country. To go there would require a four-wheel-drive vehicle. The prices were not out of line compared with gloves from other regions, so on that basis it was better to purchase them in the larger city. Also, in a larger city, you may have more of a selection of all goods as often the people from the villages bring all sorts of treasures to the larger trade centers when they need money. These items would probably not be for sale in the remote villages.

Even Europe can be a source of supply in the Importing Game, especially now that Eastern Europe has reestablished trading ties with the West. But there are fewer bargains in Europe, so you have to be a bit more clever. The prices are as high or higher than in America; the products are often similar, and more people are competing to buy European goods for export to the United States. However, it is still possible to find your special niche. You may do this by finding unusual items off the customary tourist trail, or you may find items in your specialty in flea markets. For example, we once found a beautiful Japanese sword guard (*tsuba*) among some junk in a street fair stall in London. The seller thought is was an odd, old thing and we were delighted to pay his price. In Spain we have been able to convince small but excellent producers of leather goods to make belts according to our design which have sold extremely well in the U.S. And recently in southern France we came across a very attractively designed comb being produced there. We are buying these from the wholesaler in France and will bring in a shipment of them which we think will be quite popular.

Considering our own desires, as well as product availability, is how we decide where to go. But really, it's not our choice, it's yours. You've seen how to do it. Now, where do you want to go?

Chapter 4

BEFORE YOU GO

Once you've decided where you are going and the type of things you want to import, you will need to get busy researching the items *and* the country. This can be fun—lots of fun—and the degree of your success will most likely be directly proportionate to the thoroughness of your efforts. Only you can decide how much time and energy you are willing to expend, but it's not unlikely that you will find research to be one of your favorite pastimes.

Let's start with getting to know the goods. For instance, you will want to know areas and methods of manufacture, the kinds of materials, nature of designs, and other such general information related to traditional "items" from the part of the world you plan to visit. You also will want to know the prices for which they retail, who generally buys them, how well they sell here and who else is importing them. There are several methods of obtaining this type of information. One of the most accessible and entertaining methods is to go prospecting (browsing) in the stores that sell the types of items you have chosen. Watch newspapers for display advertisements of specialty shops as well as department stores which feature imports. Check the yellow pages for import stores and make telephone inquiries concerning specific items. If you live in a city which houses a consulate or tourist office of the country you plan to visit, they may be able to provide information on where you can locate items imported from their country. Examining what is on the market here will provide you with useful information before you go and will assist you in developing the contacts you will need when you return with items to sell. You will be learning more about your prospective buyers here and may even begin to gather information for future trips, based on your research and growing knowledge of imports in general.

We found ourselves focusing for a time on hand-knitted accessories for women. Our first items came from the Middle East but through research and constant contact with stores in our area we realized that beautiful hand-knits came also from Europe, specifically Portugal. Eventually we planned a trip to Portugal based on this information, and it proved to be very successful.

Long walks in shopping areas are one of the best ways to find out what's available. It is easy to drive past an unobtrusive structure but very unlikely that you will miss it on foot. Be friendly and talk to the shopkeepers but don't believe everything they tell you. We have been told incredible stories about the background of an article, including its use, age and rarity, only to find out while visiting the country that the stories are simply not true. Compare what different people tell you about the same item. File the information away, compare it before you leave and verify it when you arrive in the country (and correct it when you get back, particularly if it is to your advantage!). Tell the people you meet that you are going on a trip and are thinking of bringing high-quality items back for resale. Take special care to dress in good taste but with an extra flair. Buyers love it and it will give them a subconscious verification of your good taste. They will want to know you better because you are an interesting person. Talk about being a world traveler. If you're young, talk about just starting out and get them interested in your future. If you're older, talk about changing careers in mid- or late life because of a conviction about the quality or beauty of the things that interest you, and catch them up in your enthusiasm. If it is to your advantage, stop in several times and they will begin to feel they really know you. They will think of you as an old friend and customer. But don't buy anything if you think you can get it for less "over there," except as a prototype; otherwise you will spend your profit before you leave!

If this type of contact is difficult for you, first go to lunch with a friend who thinks you are terrific. Then go out and make your contacts. People in shops who are not pressured by customers enjoy a "customer" who is interested and entertaining and who helps them see things in their own merchandise that they hadn't noticed. It gives them a much appreciated diversion if it doesn't interfere with their service to their paying customers.

Visit specialty stores and large department stores. Don't neglect large department stores. The buyers are a different breed but they generally buy more of an item. You may be able to develop a line of jewelry which will sell well at a specialty import store and with just a slight change will also sell to the department store buyer (who generally likes the ethnic look but not the authentic "tribal" look). Once we brought some beads back from a trip. They were wonderfully ethnic. Import and specialty boutiques loved them but we couldn't seem to connect with the larger department stores for the large order we were hoping for. One buyer finally confided to us what she honestly thought about them for her clientele. The clasp looked cheap by U.S. standards. We made a simple change that altered the appearance of the beads from "very ethnic" to that "Middle Eastern sophisticated look" and sold them.

Similarly, our Afghanistan socks sold well to department stores but they wanted the less ethnic colors, choosing instead the muted tones which they felt their customers preferred. We altered *our* buying plans to include more of those shades to assure larger orders.

If you are uncertain about where an article originates, ask the clerk (it is a good opening) to see items from her department that come from the country you will be visiting. The Federal Trade Commission labeling act for textiles assists in finding textile items from a country, as they must be clearly labeled as to country of origin. Additionally, many other non-clothing items are labeled in some way, often with a small stick-on type label stating the country of origin.

Talk with every traveler, shopkeeper and buyer you can. It will help you learn more about the products, the shops, the market and useful bits of trade gossip; it will make you a more interesting and confident person. Pretty soon you will be telling them all about merchandise and *they* will listen. You will become an expert without even leaving the country. They will tell you of other stores to visit (leads!). Just make sure that you eventually do take that trip, both for your credibility and to make use of all that information you've acquired.

Once you've determined that a certain type of item is already "around," you will want to know how it sells in its current form. Your conversations with the salespeople will help you establish that (but only if they know you are an importer, else they may tell you it sells like crazy and why don't you buy several). So take the bull by the horns and get in touch with the buyer. Find out if the item sells. If not, what changes could help it sell? Is there more demand than supply? Has that particular buyer any definite source for these items, or have they simply been purchased on a one-time basis? In many countries the difficulties of exporting and of establishing reliable sources of supply result in only a small quantity of certain items getting to the United States. Can you offer the merchandise to them at a lower price? Keep in mind always that the retail stores will mark an item up approximately one hundred percent, so gauge your negotiations with that in mind.

You may find an advantage in discussing your trip in advance with the owner, manager, or buyer in specialty boutiques and import shops. Many are looking for specific items.

They may place orders with you before you leave and actually tell you what to buy, give you exact specifications and establish a price You will then be able to figure out how much you can pay for a given item in a foreign country with the addition of duty, freight and a reasonable profit.

We learned this the hard way by returning from a trip to a remote section of the Middle East with lovely textiles. We arrived in a very well-known import shop with all of our treasures. While enthusiastic over our finds, the buyer told us she was unable to buy anything for three months. She had made a prior commitment to purchase a large group of imports from another traveler visiting another country and, therefore, had no available money to buy from us at that time. She kept saying over and over, “Why didn’t you let me know you were going?” We repeat it to you. We were particularly disgusted with ourselves since this shop was in our daily line of travel and we had looked in there many times prior to our trip to obtain pricing information but had never mentioned our proposed travels.

Another excellent way to survey what items are already available and relative prices being sought for them is to locate someone who can get you into one of the local gift, boutique, apparel or other trade shows in your area. Talk to the people who have booths there with items of the type and from the part of the world you plan to visit. They are generally friendly and helpful if they are not busy with customers. Ask them how they got started. Many may tell you that “It’s too late from that part of the world—everything’s been done.” Don’t take their word for it without double-checking. Chances are they may not want any more competition.

Once we were given a plausible and convincing description by an importer on the problems of selling lapis lazuli jewelry, including a multitude of reasons as to why we should abandon our newly developed line, and an explanation of why he was not doing jewelry himself. We became so overwhelmed with his convincing presentation that we seriously considered abandoning importing completely. Shortly thereafter we found out from a friend that the man was actually planning to offer a new line of lapis lazuli jewelry for sale in the United States, and was incorporating *our* designs in his new line!

Checking prices for different types of items is an important part of your research. Another equally essential part is learning differences in quality or detail and their effect on prices. Do you find different prices for what appears to be the same item? Is it really the same item or is the quality higher in one? Is one real silver instead of white metal, silk instead of rayon, handmade instead of machine made, or is it simply selling in a fancy department store? The point to be made is—know *why* the price is different. We were surprised once upon entering a store specializing in items from a particular country we had just visited. They had a necklace there retailing for $75. It was displayed with several other unusual looking pieces in a special display case. The same piece was retailing in a medium-priced department store in town for about $45, and we had the piece in our own line to retail for about $50. Why the price difference? We knew enough about the item to know that there was no difference in quality or design. The reason was simply that the $75 necklace was in a very fancy jewelry display case. It looked as though it should cost $75, and ultimately, it sold for $75. The department store necklace was in a standard department store case with jewelry of various sorts.

Another spectacular example was a bracelet which we found in a low- to medium-priced import specialty shop, retailing for $3.95 and the very same bracelet in a quite fancy specialty shop, where nothing would *ever* sell for $3.95. It didn't—the retail price was $37.50!

In another instance, we imported some hand-knitted slippers from the Middle East. We found such slippers were retailing in a very expensive department store for $14; a more sporty, expensive department store for $9; a specialty shop of things from that country for $7.50; and we were planning to retail ours for $10. We learned the slippers in the specialty shop were imported by the proprietor and, therefore, he was able to keep his price very low and his quality very high (as he had personally selected each one). However, he probably could not wholesale them all over the country and maintain that as a retail price. The $9 slippers were hand-carried over by a one-time importer who was planning to develop a footwear business. He may be surprised when he tries to ship and maintain this price. Also the fiber content was inferior on these slippers as compared to the others. They were acrylic while the others were wool and/or cotton. Incidentally, in addition to the country of origin, the fiber content is also required on most textile items by the Federal Trade Commission and must be accurately, completely and visibly displayed on the item. The $14 slippers were of an extremely high quality, better than any other, their fiber content was all wool, and each pair was perfect. Additionally, they were selling at a very expensive department store where the customers would expect to pay that price. One high-volume import store was supposed to be getting some to sell for $5. They never arrived because the importer's pricing structure was based on out-of-date exchange rates. He simply could not deliver for that price. What this shows is that if you could have brought similar slippers in and retailed them for somewhere between $6 and $14 you would probably have been able to sell them all, particularly if the quality was high. Moral: Know your prices and what they mean!

Now that you've started walking the streets and hopefully making some friends along the way, it is time to evaluate what type of other contacts can be made prior to your departure that may make your trip more fun and more profitable.

Sit down one evening with your traveling companion and a bottle of good wine and try to think of everyone you have ever known who has been to this part of the world. Then invite them to dinner or lunch. Don't leave out one traveling friend. Some valuable leads come this way. You can hear about the country, romanticize about it, learn how best to get around in it, maybe find out about a great hotel, exceptional shopping areas and possibly even be offered the names of some contacts they have made in that country. They may be able to give you some leads to other people who have been there and who might talk to you. This is more important than it would appear. It is often very difficult to obtain information in the United States about some of the countries where unusual purchases can be made. Oftentimes the information available at your destination may also be sketchy, so reports of experienced travelers are most useful.

Our Afghanistan socks initially were shown to us by a very experienced world traveler friend whom we invited to dinner. We were not completely convinced we actually wanted to go to Afghanistan or that we would find anything interesting to buy there. He arrived with brochures, books and socks, which he threw into the middle of our living room floor, announcing "these socks are the best thing to buy in Afghanistan—everyone will want them when you return." His enthusiasm was contagious. He was right and this was our first introduction to one of our most successful imports.

A hair appointment led to an interesting contact. Mary was at Elizabeth Arden's prior to departure on a trip and an elegant woman overheard her conversation about it and joined in the discussion. She herself had recently traveled to the country discussed. She developed into a wonderful friend, providing us with a personal letter to the American ambassador and his wife. She also owns one of the most elegant and well-known antique establishments in the area and thereafter became a customer.

We once received a name from an importer friend of someone who sold fabulous old embroideries in Afghanistan. The only problem in locating the gentleman was that one had to go to a certain part of the capital city and stand on a vaguely defined street corner and repeatedly call out his name. Eventually he would be informed and would, in due course, arrive on the scene. We did go to Afghanistan again, shortly thereafter, and while we never actually had the nerve to call out his name on a street corner, we did pursue this lead by asking other shopkeepers in the area about him. No one knew his whereabouts, or so they claimed, but when they realized that we wanted to buy items from him because we were "importers" they pulled out everything they could think of to sell us. We made some interesting contacts as a result and found some very fine merchandise. It was an opener.

On the other hand, one friend suggested that we take sleeping bags to a certain country because of the undeveloped facilities over there. It turned out that he had not been there for several years and facilities were now adequate. We were stuck with the extra bulk of sleeping bags as extra baggage for a month, and wished we had obtained a second opinion. So get as much information as you can, from as many sources as possible.

Let everyone know you are "in importing." Tell the checkout girl at the market and the new couple you meet at a party. You never know when you will meet someone who 1) will want to buy something from you later, 2) has a great contact in another country, 3) has a great contact here, or 4) will tell everyone else about this marvelous thing you are doing and you will become a sought-after personality. Additionally, the more you talk, look and listen, the more "expert" you will become and doors will open to you.

Keep your ears open! Sometimes people will give you tips or interesting things they have run across and think someone should import. We developed a most interesting import from Europe that way. So many things have come from Europe that it is difficult to develop new items at prices that are competitive with American goods. However, one evening at a party, a woman knowing of our impending trip to France spoke to us of some lovely plaster of paris replicas of the old official seals of Paris she had seen about ten years earlier. She told us how to find the remote building in Paris where they were kept. We searched them out and found them to be lovely and reasonably priced. We made them into pins and necklaces by simply gluing a pin on the back or adding a clasp and cord in the case of necklaces. Frankly, we would never have found these any other way.

In order to eliminate surprises, it is smart to take the time to contact some governmental agencies before you leave. For example, check with the appropriate federal regulatory agencies to learn whether there are any restrictions or potential problem items from the area where you are going. It could be that the sheep of some one area have a special disease and, therefore, rugs or other wool products are prohibited. Knowing this will allow you to avoid having them confiscated at the United States point of entry. We once planned to bring back from North Africa a line of stuffed camels for children. The problems turned out to be insurmountable. The camels had some sharp corners and other projections that were illegal under federal regulations relating to toys. Additionally, because they were stuffed and from a potential drug originating area, each camel was subject to the possibility of being ripped open to assure that the stuffing was really only stuffing. The situation was impossible and we had to cancel our camels.

Customs agents can be very helpful. You can check with them prior to leaving about applicable duty on items you are planning to bring back. Appendix A lists the customs districts throughout the United States so you can easily find the headquarters nearest you. Duty on some items may prohibit your being able to sell them at a reasonable profit. On other items, quotas may have been established and your item may not be allowed entry to the United States without going through a quota desk. For example, only a certain number of meters of, let us say, cotton may be allowed in the U.S. from a particular country in a given year. If this quota has been filled, you may not be able to bring back anything made of cotton for resale. Learn this *before* you go! Customs agents can help you regarding illegal items and items which may have a potential problem (i.e., scarves of certain materials may possibly be flammable and therefore subject to certain regulations).

Additionally, customs can let you know which countries are under the GSP (Generalized System of Preferences) classification, which is a preferential status because of their lack of development. (See Appendix B.) In those cases, duty is either reduced or dropped on many items and quotas do not come into consideration. But more of this in a later chapter.

It is also helpful, interesting and can make your trip more fun to have letters or personal contacts with someone who is a national of the country you will be visiting. Your friends may know someone or you may run into a contact another way. We developed such a situation quite by accident the first time. We became acquainted with a young college student from the Middle East prior to our departure. He was a charming young man and asked us to look up his parents during our stay in his country. We did so. His father was the chief prosecutor of the country and he had several relatives who were in the export business who wished to have further contacts with the United States. It developed into a most successful business situation.

The quality of our trip experience was also greatly enhanced as we spent a lot of time with these fine people in their home sharing their lives for a time. A connection with someone reliable in another country can be immeasurably beneficial not only in getting around the country and adapting to their customs more quickly, but in locating items in which you have an interest and in bargaining and fixing prices if there is a language barrier. This type of contact can also assist in assuring that your shipments are, in fact, sent. If you decide to import that item again, your overseas friend can be helpful as a contact and in the control of the quality of the exported merchandise.

Under any circumstance, do learn some of the language of the country you are visiting. The people will love it and it will help you in getting around and finding what you are looking for. Once you have found something you want to buy, it will be helpful to you in your bargaining efforts.

There are various ways to learn the language. The most obvious and most expensive are the language schools. Or you may simply buy a dictionary and some language records and "learn it in your sleep." A less expensive method and one that can prove very interesting is to find someone like yourself who will teach you the language for a reasonable fee. Call the university nearest you and talk with someone in the department covering the studies of the country you are to visit. There is often someone—a student or young professor, or friend of either—who will be glad to pick up some extra money by teaching you some of their language. Check also with specialty import shops. They may know of someone.

Or, you may wish to try one of our more successful methods. Call a restaurant specializing in food from that country and someone there may be willing, and able, to teach you the language or help you locate someone who will. One of our best contacts came about this way. We called a restaurant prior to embarking on a trip to a country with a very unusual language. The young man with whom we spoke was a waiter there. In two weeks' time he taught us enough of the language to get around and additionally asked us to look up his family over there. All the other waiters in this restaurant were from that country and asked us to do the same. Our travel experience was much improved by our contacts with these new overseas friends. We enjoyed many meals in their home. They knew wonderful, "authentic" places to go for food and entertainment. They directed us to shops and could verify the authenticity of the items we wanted.

Find out the bargaining customs before you go. How much can you normally expect to have the price reduced by bargaining and how do you do it? Are you expected to drink a lot of tea? Entertain a shouting match for several hours? Go down by increments of one hundred? Insult the man? Or highly praise him and everyone in his family whom you've never met? On one occasion, we exacted a fine bargain for some hats which took about an hour of drinking tea and discussing the personal financial plight of the merchant. It was the custom in that country, when foreigners were bargaining in the marketplace, for everyone to stand around and listen to what was going on and for the merchant to talk unceasingly with the foreigners in their language and then explain the developments, as they took place, to his friends in his own language. Quite disconcerting, but remarkable fun. There was a lot of shouting and laughing, but we got our hats for a good price.

When we initially began the research with our friends and shops, the countries we were to visit seemed so imposing. But we had lots of wonderful dinner parties with our traveling friends. We also learned so much about the shops in our area that not much had to be done for future trips, really just maintenance and updating. We still correspond with nearly everyone we met on that trip. We made many new friends over here, as everyone wants to tell about their trip. We found friends more excited about us because we were doing something different.

This all may sound like quite a lot to do just to take a simple trip. However, it really is not. Every step will not only make your purchasing more effective and efficient, but it will also improve the quality of your travel experience.

Now that you are ready to leave, consideration is needed on how to approach "over there."

Chapter 5

HOW TO BUY—IN URDU

What do we mean, "How to Buy—in Urdu"? You really don't speak Urdu you say. Well, we really didn't expect that you did unless you've lived in Pakistan. But not speaking the language won't stop you if you plan ahead and are reasonably sensitive to the situation.

It's true, when you are buying merchandise abroad, language and customs are different and it's not always simple. You ask the merchant the price of an object and what happens? He might not understand English and he may not know what you are talking about. Or he might understand your question, or guess it and respond, perhaps, with the price in Urdu! On the other hand, it might be premature in his culture to talk about price, so he might instead answer with a glowing testimonial for his product, again in Urdu. The process of making a purchase abroad can be far more complicated than at home and requires a little training.

You might remember the procedure as the 3 C's—communication, custom and care.

≈ COMMUNICATION ≈

As you can see, the ability to communicate is critical. We can attest, from many experiences, that there are few things as frustrating as having traveled halfway around the world, finding an object that you very much want to buy and being unable to determine the price. Of course, you can produce increasing amounts of cash, hoping to strike a responsive chord, but that is undesirable for two reasons. First, it might offend the seller under local custom and completely negate the deal. Worse, it is an invitation to be taken advantage of. A country tradesman may be fascinated at the display and wonder how long it can continue. His delay in responding may have nothing to do with what he thinks his goods are worth. But, once he sees it all and realizes that you would be willing to part with that sum, that's going to be his price.

One of the most valuable things you can do is to learn the numbers of the language in which you will be dealing. If you think back to your school days and language courses, you will recall that words for figures above ten can become quite complicated. But, if you use the words in a simplistic sense coupled with an awareness of the written figures, you are miles ahead. Then if you find a shop with the prices written, you will be able to make your comparisons and conversions without any assistance. You will know that ¥一六七五 means 1675 yen (¥) for the object at issue. If you are not sure, and sometimes it is hard to follow written characters, you can point to the figures and say to the clerk, "ichi" (1), "roku" (6), "shichi" (7), "go" (5) as you point to each figure in turn. If you get a "hi" (yes) then that is probably the price. Granted, this is most rudimentary and you have not really even been able to say the price in proper Japanese, but you have confirmed to yourself the figures you need to know to make the analysis for purchase.

Our suggestion in any place where your own tongue is not commonly spoken is to learn as much of the language as you practically can. At a minimum, for buying purposes, you ought to be able to ask, "How much?" be able to say and understand "yes" and "no" and be able to say and write figures from 0 to 9. (See Appendix D.) You'll find it will save you a lot of frustration and make things considerably easier. You might also wish to learn a few polite and formal forms of address, and it would be desirable to learn how to avoid familiar verbs and pronouns. These are usually reserved for intimate friends, relatives, servants and children in other parts of the world, particularly in Europe.

It is also invaluable, in fact, almost imperative to have one of those small pocket dictionaries with you. It can often help you out of the complete frustration of noncommunication. If you are unable to find one to bring along (for some more exotic languages they are very difficult to locate here) pick one up over there and be sure to keep it. Bring it back and add it to your growing dictionary library! For quick reference, the pam phlets or booklets of phrases distributed by the airlines or national tourist offices may be helpful.

Or, you may wish to invest in a language computer. They have keyboards with the letters of the alphabet in English, into which you put your phrase. The result, in the language of your choice, shows up on a small screen. They are nearly small enough to hold in your hand, and some of them even talk to you. We haven't personally had experience with them yet, but you may wish to investigate.

If things get too complicated, great assistance can be found at times from the nearest available person who speaks your language. We have on numerous occasions been rescued in our negotiations by the passing stranger or the neighboring shopkeeper. Sometimes the interpreter is someone who has learned your language and is grateful for an opportunity to practice it and to be of assistance to you both. Other times, however, the serendipitous stranger is part of the seller's usual routine and your interpreter is not a neutral friend, but an agent of the seller. Be careful that you aren't so relieved at his appearance that you bare your soul and negotiating strategy. On the other hand, too much caution on your part may dampen the enthusiasm of a real Samaritan and turn him into an ally of the seller.

The best solution usually is to be pleased and friendly with the fortuitous interpreter. Engage him in conversation and try, during the course of it, to sense the neutrality of the intermediary. It is hard, and you don't always guess right, but it's the best you can do. Resume the negotiations in a friendly fashion, but reveal your position and advance your bids in light of that assessment.

It is hard to overemphasize the importance of communication. Many Americans have had little to do with other languages or customs. English is so widely spoken it is possible for Americans to travel in many parts of the world and to understand and be understood enough so that their linguistic incapacities do not seriously disadvantage them. There is no better example of how we take communication for granted than when we tried to meet someone at an office in Tokyo on our first trip to Japan.

A friend deposited us in front of the appropriate building and we entered. A quick glance at the building directory let us know we were in trouble. It was all in Japanese characters! Thinking we recollected the appropriate floor we decided to chance it and get on the elevator. When we went to push "14" we couldn't tell which button was "14." Our friend was in the building above us but we didn't know how to get to him. We tried to ask for assistance from some people in the lobby but no one could understand us. And we couldn't even tell our friend that we had arrived because we couldn't find him in the Japanese-character phone book. Eventually we had to leave without seeing him.

We did, however, learn the lesson that a bit of preparation in a foreign environment can make a substantial difference. Now, we would have a Japanese friend or one of the staff at the information desk of our hotel write the name of the company and the person in Japanese characters on a piece of paper so we could show it to people from whom we sought directions. And we would have had his phone number with us so we could telephone and apprise him of our plight. Similarly, in Japan and some other places it is useful to have your hotel address written out in the local language so that you can at least show it to a cab driver to help get you back.

We've noticed, too, that the problems of communication cause Americans to get frustrated and impatient. Often that results in their talking more, faster and louder. That is not what you want to do! The more you talk, the less you listen, and what you are trying to do is pick up the signals of what these other people are trying to say. Talking loudly and impatiently may be discourteous in their culture and will reduce your ability to gain their assistance and cooperation.

Most foreigners are aware that we Americans are friendly and informal. But it is wise to moderate these qualities when abroad. Over there we are foreigners and their guests, and too much friendliness and familiarity may be misunderstood as a lack of respect. Don't expect all foreigners to appreciate Ameri can humor, and avoid touching anyone except to shake hands.

First names are almost never used except by very close acquaintances, and definitely not at the time of first meeting as in the U.S.

Even your European counterparts who seem culturally so close are much more formal in their behavior and language (in spite of any superficial indication to the contrary).

It is important for women to remember that the roles of women and the behavior which is acceptable for women may be very different in some countries. Independent attitudes on the part of women will not help in most developing countries. In some countries, women's status is so low that the cattle receive more attention and concern. Foreign women are often considered fascinating, but not really taken seriously when it comes to business transactions. However, work it to your advantage. Once while bargaining for a pair of trousers, the merchant kept greeting Mary with a kiss on each cheek. Each time he greeted her, she continued bargaining and cut her offering price by half. Eventually she got the trousers that started out at seven dollars for one dollar, and everyone was happy. Don't feel that you are letting yourself down by accepting the help of a man; it is necessary in some countries.

≈ CUSTOMS OF THE MARKET ≈

Certainly every marketplace has its own customs and all parties should adhere to them, including yourself. On the other hand, it's hard to know what they are. For that reason, we always think it's a good idea to spend at least one day observing what's happening and making some reasoned conclusions about the patterns of acceptable behavior.

Watch what the locals do. Do they walk into a shop, pick a particular product, pay for it and leave? Do you find that they seem to engage in a long discussion? Does it appear to be bargaining? Does it seem necessary to sit down for tea before discussing business? If there are bigger stores and smaller markets, do the patterns seem different between the two types of sales outlets? Watch how much the locals pay for a product of the sort that interests you.

Once you've watched a bit and think you know the price of an object that's of interest to you, dip your toe in the water. Make a small purchase and see if the pattern is compatible with your expectations. This is the perfect opportunity to buy the little gift for Aunt Lillian or Uncle Harry. Instead of buying a piece of tourist junk at the airport you will have an unusual item and probably a good story to go with it. You will have perfected your awareness of this particular market, and gained an insight into the society as a whole, for the patterns that people follow in their commerce say a lot about how they view life. Does life consist of friendly or impersonal relationships? Are people rushed or relaxed in their buying habits? Do people want to be taken at their word or tested? You'll learn a lot by watching.

If you've learned that the pattern is to bargain, then you should start bargaining right away. Start with the small purchases and get used to testing the limits when the item to be purchased doesn't mean that much to you. It will make it easier to do when the price is greater. If bargaining is the pattern, you must do it, too, for several reasons. If you're just a tourist buying a few trinkets for yourself and if you'll never deal with these people again, perhaps you can say you prefer not to bargain. You'll only have lost a little money and an interesting experience. But if you are going to succeed in the Importing Game, you have to bargain. If you don't, you will pay too much, and if you are going to be reselling those objects, that extra amount might be the difference between a salable product and one that's priced over the market. Any competitor of yours who does bargain will be able to undersell you.

Also, your seller will have less respect for you. Bargaining societies are usually quite competitive and successful competitors are respected. You will want to build the respect of your sellers so that they will offer you their better products and deal with you more fairly. So, you've got to bargain!

One day in Bali, we came across a beautiful painting. It was of that very detailed, complicated sort in naturalistic greens and browns. It was in a shop which catered to tourists and which was stocked almost entirely with cruder variants of the same type of painting. The shopkeeper kept trying to steer us away from this picture in favor of the cheaper, cruder tourist fare. We persisted in our interest and eventually were quoted a price of $275 U.S. We started at $100 and almost walked out before he took our final offer of $150. We thought it was a fine enough work to warrant the $275 price, but we knew from watching the Balinese merchants that bargaining was the game. We may be wrong, but we had the feeling that the seller preferred seeing that work go to someone who bargained for it.

We can't tell you how to bargain, but we can give you a few tips from our experience.

1. *Know your top price.* Bargaining, like any contest, is best done if you know what your goal is. Remember that in bargaining theory, your first response to the seller's offer sets the bargaining range. The ultimate price is unlikely to be lower than the first figure you state and will probably be near the midpoint between the seller's offer and your response. So think carefully about that first response. Without a predetermined goal, you'll probably agree as soon as the seller accepts the first counteroffer. Most bargaining societies have general rules of thumb which you ought to be able to guess by watching some transactions. In Bali, for example, the general range of transactions was at about half the asking price. So, when we were told $275, we immediately dropped to under one half the asking price to provide room for compromise at the expected figure. We probably should have gone lower at first but felt somewhat embarrassed to suggest such a low price. That was probably a mistake. Had we liked the work less and been a bit harder in our attitude we would probably have offered $75 and gone up to $125. We figured that the acceptable price range was probably between $125 and $150. We had resolved not to pay more than that. So when he met our price, we didn't bargain further—and considering how we started our bidding probably were foreclosed from doing so then.

2. *Keep your eye on what you really want.* It is a usual tactic for a seller to try to confuse you and divert you by showing you other alternatives at different prices. These alternatives are designed usually to convince you that the price he is proposing for the object at issue is certainly reasonable or that if you want to spend less there are these other items which are almost as good, and these others that are better for more. The psychology is probably that you will get into a pattern of thinking of the proposed prices as the reasonable range rather than the actual lower expected price. It also gives the seller a means of

sizing you up as a negotiator. How strongly you keep coming back to the one you originally selected gives the seller a gauge of how much you want that piece and the reasons. He uses this in establishing his later counter-offers.

There is one other aspect to the merchant's game of running you through the alternatives. Sometimes a seller has a particularly fine piece which you have examined carefully before you made your first proposal. The seller may have other such pieces which are similar, but not quite as good. After confusing you with many better and lesser alternatives, if the seller suspects your choice of that original piece was not as informed as was first thought, he may finally show you not the piece you first looked at, but its lesser cousin. You'll get it back to the hotel and find a crack or a repair that you don't remember seeing when you were examining it in the shop.

Know then what you want, and know why you want it, but don't give the seller the information that he wants to gauge why you want it. Be noncommittal and even somewhat bored. Don't give the impression that it matters to you, even if the piece is unique and you want it badly. It's like a poker game. Keep up the bluff.

But keep your eye on the particular piece you've selected; consider alternatives that you might not have seen, but don't be swayed by them and don't let a carefully selected piece be replaced by another while your attention is diverted.

3. *The tactical withdrawal.* In Bali, we were about to walk out when the seller finally agreed to a price which was our predetermined maximum. This is something you have to do at times. A seller will sometimes not believe your bluff of nonchalance. But when he sees you walk out the door and up the street he realizes that you are not going to settle on other terms, no matter how much you might really want it. The way to good negotiating is to be willing to let anything go.

We have had sellers test us to the point of letting us walk out and down the street. Then, they have run after us and made a counteroffer or accepted our last proposal. So be prepared to walk out. The seller will respect you for it and will be pleased to resume negotiations on your return.

Use all your wits in the negotiating game. The sellers are.

≈ CAREFUL — MAKE SURE ≈ YOU GET IT AFTER YOU'VE BOUGHT IT

It's easy to think, after you've made your deal, that you can relax and be friends with the seller. Often you can, but sometimes you get surprised.

We once thought we bought some elegant coats in Kabul, Afghanistan, after some spirited bargaining. We were pleased to have gotten such good pieces at such a favorable price. We were leaving the next day for the northern part of the country and did not want to lug the coats along with us so we told the merchant that we would pick them up in five days. When we returned after that trip the merchant disclaimed any knowledge of our prior deal. The coats were nowhere to be seen in his shop. We were angry and puzzled. Some months later in a San Francisco import shop we found those same coats. Apparently someone else had come upon the same merchant in that five-day period and offered a more attractive price. But unlike us, they had taken the coats with them. The moral of that story is obvious. When you've made your deal, pay the price and take your purchases. That stops further negotiations or mysterious disappearances.

And when we suggest you take it with you, that means then. Don't be careless. Many people have been surprised when unwrapping their purchases on their return home to find that what they bought doesn't look as good as they remember. Sometimes it's true that the magic of a moment adds uniqueness to an otherwise unexceptional piece. But sometimes it doesn't look as good because it isn't. It's the old backroom switch again. After you've made your deal, watch the wrapping process. Don't do it in a suspicious way, but keep your eye on what's happening.

We happened in on the end of one trying experience when an American couple had purchased an outstanding old tapestry for $150. While negotiating they had noticed a large spot on the tapestry. The merchant assured them he could easily have it cleaned and he was very convincing. They paid him and later returned to pick up their purchase. As it turned out, one of the colors had run all over the rest of the tapestry during the merchant's cleaning process, ruining it. They had already paid for it and the merchant simply said, "It is yours." Finally, after about an hour, they convinced him to let them have another item as a substitute. When they left he turned to us and told us with glee that the final item they took was only worth about $60 and he had profited by the additional $90. Needless to say, we did not deal with him.

The merchant may offer to mail it to you. Many people have never received the goods that were mailed, nor have they gotten acknowledgments to their letters sent to the seller. A word to the wise should be sufficient. Unless you know you can trust the seller, mail it yourself. We'll describe the details later. We also know of one man who paid for a large purchase which was to be sent to him. When he got home he got another bill from the seller stating he could not send the items until he received an additional amount of money as he had miscalculated the amount!

≈ CAREFUL — WATCH YOUR ≈ REACTIONS

You know how moods can affect your efficiency. Did you ever think about how they affect your shopping? If you are shopping professionally, as you will be in the Importing Game, you have to watch your reactions.

Once we were buying an Imari bowl in Japan. We were in a shop that had hundreds of beautiful bowls, many antique and all beautiful. They must have had over fifty of the size and general quality and age we were seeking. We would pick, then reject, then pick another only to have that superseded by a new discovery. We got so engrossed in selecting the best combination of design and color that we spent an hour and a half selecting one bowl. We had it wrapped and brought it home. Only then did we notice that the bowl was off center; in fact it was lopsided. It may have had the very best design, but its shape was so bad that the bowl was really worth much less than we had paid for it. What had gone wrong? It was no one's fault but our own. We had allowed ourselves to get distracted by one element of the design—to lose sight of the total object.

We can easily be distracted, we can be diverted by extraneous factors. It is important to ask yourself from time to time whether this really is as good as you think, will it really sell back home.

Saturation is another enemy of good buying. We were buying some other bowls in Kyoto. We had been on that particular trip for about two weeks at the time, looking at bowls every day. Late one day we found a shop which had nothing but high-quality bowls. We were there for about an hour looking at one group and another when suddenly we felt so sick of bowls we almost left, without buying anything. We sat down, talked about it, regained our perspective, settled on the nicest ones we could find and bought them. They proved to be even better than they seemed at the time. Sometimes saturation is the necessary first step to a fully considered choice. Again, step back and reconsider. Don't act on the basis of your feelings of the moment.

Another emotional reaction which can be engendered in bargaining is antagonism. Haughty or uncaring salespeople can also create antagonism. In bargaining it is most serious because it may cause you to give away your position in anger or to speed the bargaining to a conclusion to rid yourself of the vexation. Remember that there are some bargainers who purposefully attempt to anger or rattle you so you lose control of the situation. Don't let them get to you.

More common is the merchant who takes you into his confidence, befriends you, so that you let your defenses drop. Some years ago when we were going to Hong Kong regularly on business we would stop in to chat with a dealer of oriental antiquities at a spot not far from our hotel. He told us many things about Chinese ceramics and in time we began to trust in his advice and in his good intentions. Finally one day we bought a Sung dynasty bowl. As circumstances would have it, our life pattern changed then and we didn't return to Hong Kong for a while. In the interval we had other occasions to learn about Chinese ceramics and came to learn that many of the things he had told us were erroneous and our initial purchase of Chinese ceramics was not a good one. We made the error of letting affection and friendship cloud our judgment. We didn't independently check what he told us. If we had we would have realized that at best his knowledge was not as great as we had assumed it to be and at worst, well, you know. The lesson? Be friendly, be willing to listen and to learn from others but don't let your decisions be clouded by the comfortable feeling that your friend knows best. There are commercial friendships, but some such friends don't care whether the friendship lasts beyond the first sale.

So, keep your wits about you. Don't be afraid to buy, but do keep in mind your checklist to avoid purchases based on hasty or overly emotional decisions.

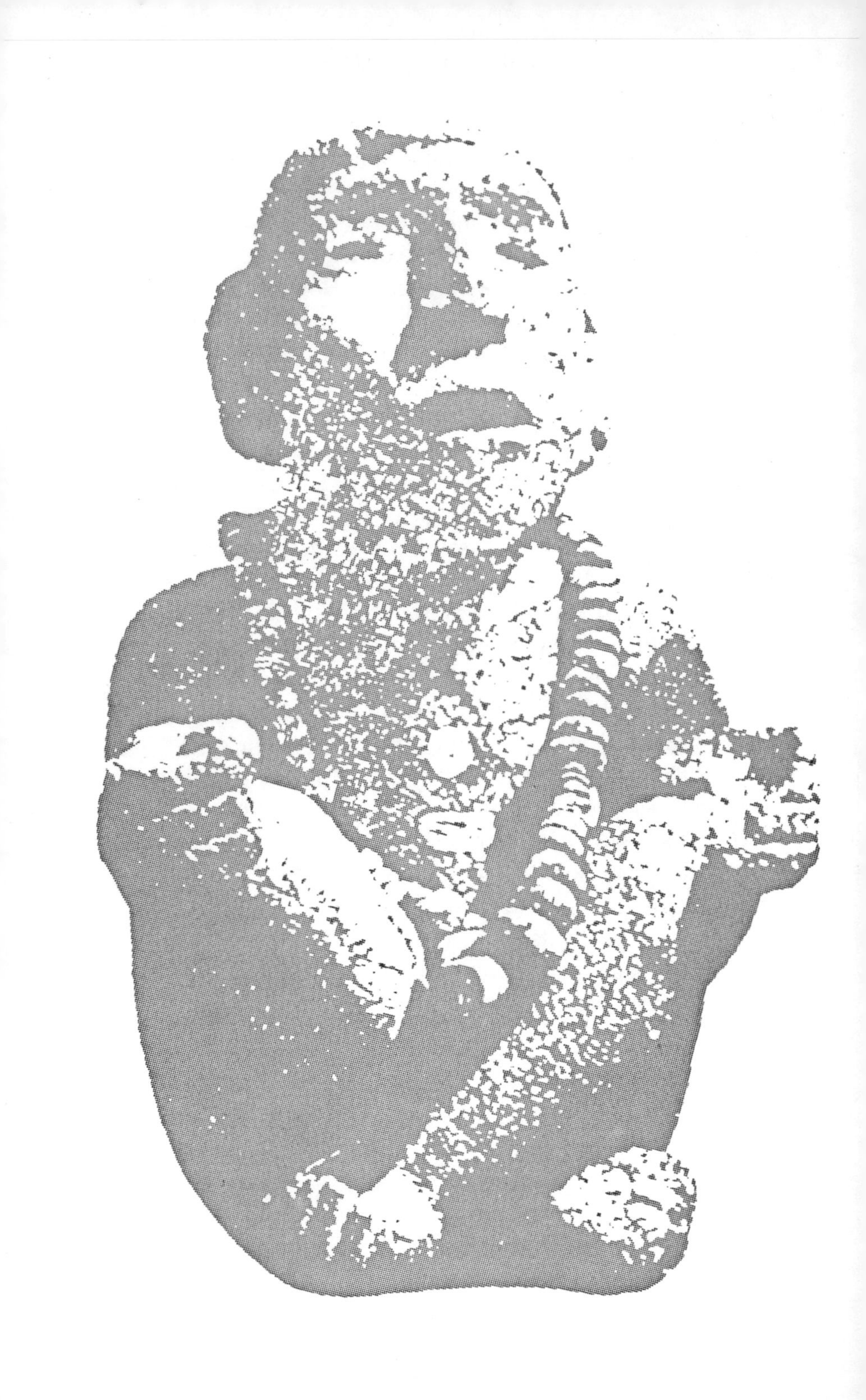

Chapter 6

CREATIVE BUYING

A young woman visiting West Africa discovered some outstanding fabrics. The craftsmanship applied to the fabrics was strikingly skillful and time consuming. But she was less than enthusiastic about the color combinations, feeling they were not appealing to her and would probably not be good for the American market. Most people would have settled for silent admiration. But she put her painting background to work, adapting the traditional techniques and designs for a contemporary Western market. The result is a far-flung cottage textile industry which provided a market for authentic African fabrics with altered color schemes by incorporating them in fashions designed and sewn in the United States.

The fabrics are made into table linens, clothing and are used in interior design. They sell to some of the most prestigious stores in the United States and the woman is now developing a South American market. She engaged in a bit of creative buying in the Importing Game. She developed something new by a little personal designing, and by using materials other than as originally intended by the makers.

Some of your most salable items may be those purchased with creative thought concerning possible other uses, modifications, combinations of articles, or entire new designs. Many have brought back various things from trips which were intended for a use other than that to which it was put at home. Haven't we all complimented, or been complimented, on the "creative" use of an item? And didn't others want one too? Have you ever requested that some article of clothing be slightly altered to suit you better before purchasing it? That was your first step toward designing.

There are a number of categories of creative buying. They overlap somewhat, but let us attempt to define and illustrate each individually.

≈ WHAT ELSE CAN YOU ≈ USE IT FOR?

Our foreign Christmas ornament line was born when we were inspired by traditional hair ornaments worn by peasant women in one section of the world. We purchased all we could get from the marketplace, about one hundred, for around 60 cents each. They later sold in a well-known Christmas ornament shop. We made $140 by indulging ourselves in a bit of creative buying. No one had ever seen this Christmas ornament before! We developed a reasonable reorder business for them as they were "truly unique," and we had the beginning of our foreign Christmas ornament line.

We had always heard that "everything had already been done for the American market." Of course that is not so! But even by using what has been done already or been around but in a different way or for a different purpose, we were, and you will be, able to develop potentially salable items that are new to the market.

We continued to add to our Christmas ornament line by considering whether small items which we ran across all over the world could hang on a tree with little or no modification, thereby transforming them into new types of Christmas ornaments. Often they are small toys in their country of origin. We took a small decorative toy shoe, added a metal hanging ring and had another lovely Christmas ornament. Two toy leather shoes draped over a tree branch with their connecting string became another such ornament. In an area in Mexico, very small, fully clothed dolls made of cloth are a traditional craft. They made marvelous, unique ornaments.

We took colorful socks made by the workmen in a remote section of Iran and sold them as Christmas stockings. They were very bright in reds and greens and looked like Christmas. One year we took the knee-high knitted socks of the Paghman and Bamiyan areas of Afghanistan and sold them as Christmas stockings in both adult and children's sizes, resulting in a considerable profit during one season.

Lovely pieces of fabric, hand-painted, embroidered, or otherwise ornamented can be hemmed and sold as scarves, beach cover-ups, table runners, or framed and sold as decorative works of art. Our Tunisian scarf purchase would have sold more quickly had we found a way of having each signed by the maker. The market at the time was for designer-signed items. So if you are able to purchase hand painted items from the original makers, be sure to have him or her sign them; you then have a "designer-signed" scarf or an original "signed" work of art.

Continually ask yourself what types of items you have seen selling in stores recently. Can something you have seen while traveling fill a need in that market? The very interesting and effective use of a traditional belt from Fez, Morocco, was as a head ornament and body jewelry as well as a belt. We probably would not have considered this use except for the fact that our research showed all sorts of body jewelry, which these belts resembled, selling in stores. To further illustrate, consider socks and soft-soled boots to be worn not under shoes but as slippers for the expanded American footwear market. We have found this type of item in Portugal, Iran, Spain, China and Afghanistan. The environmental concerns which have caused us to turn down our thermostats have also sent the consumer to the marketplace in search of new ideas in warm coverings for feet and other parts of their bodies.

You could develop a line of pillows from fabric with labels which tell the story of the circumstances under which you purchased each fabric. Call it "pillow talk." Or even make a group of shirts, blouses or children's jumpers, one-of-a-kind items, from the fabrics you find with tags "telling the story." We know of a quite successful designer of women's fashion who uses bits and pieces of interesting cloth from all over the world in his dresses. With the dress when it is sold is a card relating the story of the origin of the fabric in the dress.

Lovely metal boxes can be converted into ashtrays. Other interesting boxes and baskets from various parts of the world can make very desirable letter boxes and containers for pencils, kitchen utensils, bathroom accessories, and many other things. Consider shells as lovely soap dishes. Large baskets make interesting laundry hampers. We have also used large shells as serving dishes and ashtrays.

All sorts of interesting containers such as jars and bottles can be made into lamps. Once we even saw a samovar made into a lamp. And with a bit more work to construct a base, almost any interestingly shaped artifact can be so used.

Bowls and wastebaskets of certain types make lovely planters or plant holders. We were once given a commission by a friend to bring her back several of a particular type of wooden, hand carved wastebasket. We made a small profit. She did much better. She sold them not as wastebaskets, for which there is quite a limited market, but as plant holders with plants in them to coincide with our booming American houseplant market. They were perfect and we wished we had thought of this clever use of an ordinary item.

Birdcages of interesting shapes and materials are produced in many parts of the world. They are useful not only for housing your pet canary, but they are quite a spectacular plant holder.

Some of the most stunning old jewelry from the Middle East started out as something else, such as the head ornament for a camel or other beast of burden! In reviewing an item for possible purchase, consider all its uses- -even the less obvious ones.

One of the most interesting stories we have heard of "other use" occurred in China. In a rural commune just outside Shanghai a group of American tourists visited a shop which sold local handicrafts. A few of them discovered in a back corner what proved to be a group of "night soil" pots—wooden buckets with cast-iron handles that are used to hold human waste for later use as fertilizer. The perplexed shopkeeper asked why the Americans would want such things. The explanation that the pots could be used as planters, ice buckets or waste paper baskets seemed to only confuse him. One can only imagine the local reaction to a group of Americans strolling down a country road swinging their new "honey pots"!

≈ CAN IT BE MODIFIED? ≈

When we originally saw our elegant evening cape abroad, it was worn by a man. It was striking and so fascinating that we felt there must be some way to use it. But we felt that its greatest market in the United States would probably not be to men. So we made the simple modification of taking about five inches off the sleeve and hemming it, after which we felt it had a lot of potential for women. We purchased thirty and sold them all for a profit, adding enough to our future trip fund to pay for our hotel and food.

A major problem with this type of buying is that one can get carried away with the proposed modifications and either 1) purchase something which must be almost totally remade to be usable (you are not a manufacturer after all!), 2) the modifications are so costly or time consuming that you really will not in fact make them, or 3) the modification changes the item so much that it is no longer interesting or salable.

There are a number of garments for men in other countries which can be easily modified to accommodate women. This is a general category of good potential because in many other countries the festive dress of men is quite decorative in contrast to the somberness of formal men's clothing in our culture. Also, men in many other cultures are physically smaller than here, so that their clothing will more easily fit American women. For example, we purchased four traditional heavily ornamented antique wedding coats which had been worn by men in Turkestan. While they sell here for $300 and up in retail stores, we sold ours to our friends for $125 each, still making a reasonable profit while giving our friends a real bargain. Only a slight modification was necessary which did not substantially change the looks of the coat and was a fairly easy step.

Another interesting alteration which we have seen was quite an extensive but successful one. The traditional women's garment in Afghanistan is a pleated piece of silk which covers them from the top of their head to their toes. One trading company had them taken apart and put back together in a beautiful way to create an exotic blouse.

As an aside, let us offer a word of caution with respect to clothing from other countries. Americans are large people relative to most of the rest of the world. Make sure of your sizing. Many items from other parts of the world are too small for most of the American market. We have a friend who purchased one of the Turkestan coats from another source and she was stuck with it because it was simply too small for anyone here.

Also, do not buy only in your own size. This is a pattern almost everyone tends to fall into. Buy smaller and larger sizes for resale. We think one of the best bits of advice that we can give you is to carry a cloth tape measure with you so that you can, on the spot, check the length, bust size, sleeve length (very important) and across the shoulder measurements. Before you leave you may wish to measure some standard sizes here and carry those measurements with you to compare your own tape measure findings.

We found lovely ethnic coats once, all of which had very short sleeves (a common problem) and narrow shoulders. This was fine for the people in the originating country, but too small for Americans. We thought it strange that the length was just right but then we found out that they were floor length on the people over there, while they hit just below the knee on us!

Because this is such a difficult and recurrent problem and has caused us and so many we know countless difficulties, we are including a schedule of relative sizes, as Appendix C, for your assistance.

Footwear sizes are also a problem. Our socks from Afghanistan and Iran were stretch socks and, therefore, sizing was not crucial, but other footwear items with a definite sole require more care. We did purchase some leather slippers once which *we* sold; however, our customer told us sometime later that *he* had been unable to sell them very well. They did not stretch and, while we had sold him these slippers in a variety of sizes, even the largest size was very small for an American foot. Here your tape measure can also help. Measure standard sizes and make a note of them, not just the length, but also the width, of each size. We have also found that head sizes vary radically. Some caps we ordered did not sell because they would not fit American adults, only children. Measure a few heads and you will come up with some general conclusions.

The tape measure can also be very useful with regard to items other than clothing. If you take measurements with you of standard heights of chairs, desks, drawer depths, doorways, etc., you are better equipped to decide whether adaptive uses of articles you find are practical. For example, will a usual-size American garden pot fit into the container you're thinking of buying for a plant pot?

You may be able to take some traditional jewelry and modify it ever so slightly to make it different and, therefore, more appealing as well as marketable as a unique item. We developed a line of traditional glass beads from Pakistan. While these beads sold well, we were unhappy with the clasp and the cording, which were quite crude. We changed the original to some popular cording in bright colors to match the beads. We then had a unique piece of jewelry. It sold to quite a different market than the traditional corded beads, thereby expanding our own market.

Consider different uses for the traditional hats of a country. With some alteration, perhaps they could be made popular here by adding a band, feathers, or some fur to make them more appealing in our market. If they are stiff and ornamented we have seen them turned upside down and, with a strap added, sold as evening bags. Another interesting use of them would be to line them with plastic and use them as plant containers.

On one occasion our modifications went a bit further. We once took the knee-high socks which we sold as Christmas stockings and reaped substantial benefits during the footwear craze by having the makers: 1) remove the entire foot area, thus making a leg warmer, 2) lengthen the top part, making it a thigh-high sock, 3) add a leather sole to make a slipper or "mukluk," 4) remove the leg section and leave only the bottom as a low slipper, and 5) remove the section from the knee to the ankle to make an anklet.

We made substantial profits during the first season and had a large reorder business for years after. The people who make them still call the leg warmer, for which they have nothing similar in their country, "socks without soles."

Another interesting find were some marvelous water pipe tops in Isfahan, Iran. They were hand turned on a lathe out of lovely wood in a most unusual design. We cut off the bottom area and, lo and behold, we had some absolutely stunning candle holders.

We also know of someone who purchased lovely place mats while traveling and, upon her return, converted them into stylish evening bags which sold well.

In Indonesia we met someone who was having a batik pattern done with a rectangular center and two smaller complementary squares on each side. He was going to have the material cut and hemmed to create a place mat and four napkins.

A word on finding substitutes to make some of these modifications. Because you will be selling your goods, you should be able to purchase many needed items for alterations, i.e., cording, fabric, fasteners, at wholesale prices in the trade marts in your area. They can usually be found in the yellow pages of the telephone book listed under the type of items you are looking for identified as wholesale or by asking a knowledgeable friend (one who has a store perhaps). In many states and cities, entrance to these marts is open only to bona fide businesses and often a business card is a prerequisite for registration and entrance. So, why not have some cards made up? The cost is nominal and it could simply have your name, address, telephone number and state "Importing."

In many states you may be required to have a license or other exemption from retail sales tax in order to purchase at wholesale. In California, for example, you are required to have a resale number from the State Board of Equalization. This means you do not have to pay applicable sales tax on items to be incorporated in your modifications because you are using the goods you are purchasing in an item which will be resold to a store and the tax will be paid by the ultimate consumer. You will need to check these rules as they apply in your own area.

≈ COULD IT BE PART OF ≈ SOMETHING ELSE?

Can you frame it, hang it on the wall or from the ceiling? Could you market it in combination with other things to create a new product? A group of ceramic pieces from different sources may become a lovely collection, including possibly a cup, saucer, plate, etc. Small baubles of almost any kind can be used to decorate pillows, or the baubles themselves may be sold to bead or craft shops, or made into Christmas ornaments.

Those little Mexican cloth dolls we mentioned sold not just as Christmas ornaments. We took a French T-shirt (which we obtained at a wholesale price from the French company handling them), added a pocket in the middle, put in two dolls and enjoyed success with the sale of hundreds of them to a major department store.

One of our own most successful imports in this category combined a handsome gold lacquer box from Japan with a belt buckle from Spain and interchangeable beltings. This was put together as a gift package and sold with a gold tie around it, very successfully!

Textiles may be used as tablecloths, cushions, napkins, framed as "pictures," and in clothing. We have a friend who has collected in her travels marvelous bits and pieces of fabrics and ornaments of all sorts. She also purchases piece goods and baubles from import stores and from her friends who travel. Finding herself divorced at fifty years of age and without occupation, she has combined her collection of fabric and beads with her latent creative talent and incorporated them into designer dresses and blouses which she makes and sells for $400 to $1200 each. She now makes a very substantial income. The dresses are of simple basic design, but the use of the unusual fabrics is outstandingly creative and beautiful.

The same type of thing can be done with jewelry. In many countries you are no longer allowed to bring out old pieces of jewelry, but pieces of stone, old tassels, antique coins or other baubles, almost any small, interesting thing can be combined after arrival home to make interesting and unique jewelry for sale. We have many friends who have purchased bits and pieces this way, planning ultimately to put together a necklace for themselves. Next time, instead of keeping it yourself, try selling it to a friend!

A well-known San Francisco designer began her now lucrative business by buying both new and antique pieces on her trips to far-off places. She combined them with beads and other ornaments to make various kinds of jewelry. When she ran out of old pieces, she found and used the newer interesting pieces. Becoming more fearless, with time and success, she began to have some pieces reproduced in quantity. She is not only a successful example of modification and making it part of something else, but also of our next topic, "Your Own Designs? Why Not!"

≈ YOUR OWN DESIGNS? ≈ WHY NOT!

Could there be lurking within you the desire to be a jewelry designer, clothing designer or designer of any other kind? If the country you visit has labor which is inexpensive and the craftsmanship is of a high standard, why not try a few of your own designs?

We developed a group of stone pendants in Afghanistan which were truly unique. They were made up for us in less than a week. We developed this contact while bargaining with a merchant on other things and telling him that we were interested in exporting to the United States. He was very helpful and assisted us greatly in discovering the ins and outs of doing business in his unusual country. After the pendant designs were created, we numbered each design and developed a price for each. We made arrangements to reorder if we wished. We should emphasize at this point that in doing reorder business, be sure you are dealing with someone who is a businessperson, who understands the concepts of orders and the responsibilities of delivery and reliability. Nearly every merchant will tell you that they are "exporters." However, realize that the concept of business practices in many countries is quite different from those practiced in the United States.

We know of a woman who visited Taiwan and found the standard of wood carving so superior that she designed some wooden purses which she had executed there and imported here. We have some friends who became acquainted with a Spanish artist. They asked him if he would paint small reproductions of the great masters on some fairly ordinary large ceramic plates. They are truly unusual. Our friends won't sell them, but they could.

Clothing is another item which can be designed in many areas of the world and made up before you leave. We have previously discussed the dangers relative to the sizes in clothing. There are other reasons as well why clothing is difficult. For one thing, it is modish. A design which might be popular today in the United States may not sell by the time the design is produced and shipped. Further, a lot of clothing is seasonal and you have to sell it to the stores at the time they are stocking clothes of a full season. Also, the quality control in other parts of the world can be quite difficult to monitor from a distance. You may be stuck there yourself just to make sure everything turns out well. But in some countries it can work very well, providing reliable production of good quality. Certainly Korea, Hong Kong, and Taiwan are good. In Morocco, because of their years of dealing with the French designers, a marvelous clothing manufacturing business exists which can copy your own designs or design for you, charging extremely reasonable prices for outstanding quality. You also sometimes find this kind of situation in unexpected places. We found a marvelous manufacturing situation in London run by a Moroccan. He could copy anything and had low prices and very high quality.

A friend of ours designed fabric in Morocco and had it woven by an old craftsman to his specifications. The beautiful end product was sewn by him into his own "one of a kind" creations.

We have designed vests and sweaters out of the Afghanistan sock material. Initial reaction is very positive. Could it be that from one sock we have progressed to designers? Why not? And so can you!

≈ DON'T BE AFRAID ≈

Making something ordinary into something unique not only takes imagination, it also takes a bit of guts.

One discouraging example of our lack of courage occurred in Marrakech, Morocco. We had found some fabulous Berber decorations made of very colorful yarn, which were priced at about 20 cents each. We were in the part of the traditional marketplace which dealt in yarn goods. We saw there were literally thousands of these lovely things of varying types, all unbelievably handsome. There were reliable packing and shipping facilities within a mile of the market so we could have shipped them easily. We conservatively purchased about ten for resale as belts. It is not difficult to calculate that even if we doubled our money and sold them for 40 cents each or tripled it and sold them for 60 cents each, that would not go very far towards our trip fund. We were certain to be able to at least get our initial investment from them, anyone would have purchased them for 20 cents; therefore, we were pretty much assured of losing no money at all. Upon our return we found out that these lovely yarn decorations sold as belts for about $5 apiece retail, which would have meant that we could have sold them wholesale for around $2.50 apiece. We also found out that there was a very large demand for them at that time in retail stores, and supplies were inadequate over here. Additionally, each of our friends wanted several. This item could also have been purchased to be used by interior designers to make room dividers which we have seen since. They could have been worn as hair decorations, belts, necklaces, or added to our Christmas ornament line. An unfortunate error in judgment, but one from which we learned a great deal. When we returned to this part of Morocco several years later, the belts were still there. They were just as beautiful, but not so reasonably priced, and there was no longer the same good market for them in the United States.

If you feel sure of your ability to foresee market trends, you should keep your eyes open for items that are "sleepers" for just that reason. Our earlier cinch belt example is relevant here. Wide cinch belts were not selling in the U.S. when we originally found them in Spain. Almost all belts were very narrow, rope-like arrangements. However, we felt confident that a wider belt would become popular within six months, to help pull the volumes of fabric together on the new current styles. This did happen. We had forecast the market. We recommend this creative approach to your purchasing only if you feel *very* confident about your ability to foresee market trends!

So keep in mind that all things are not necessarily as they seem. Consider other uses, easy modifications, making it a part of something else and ultimately doing your own thing—designs!

≈ CREATIVE APPROACHES ≈ FOR SUPPLY

How do you find interesting things? What if you see something and you want more of it? How do you find out who makes it and how you can get it wholesale and possibly in quantity? By using a creative approach you should be able to find nearly anything you want.

There are some things you can do before you leave to assure you some success in finding merchandise and getting the best wholesale price (if that is within the selling structure of the country). First of all, as we suggested, you should have a business card made. It gives you a certain credibility. It is easier to have it made here than overseas. Also, some airlines will have it reprinted in the language of the country you are visiting for a very nominal cost. Or, in addition to English, you may wish to have them imprinted on the reverse side in the language of the country you will be visiting.

If you have found something and wish to know where it comes from in a particular country, we suggest that you contact the nearest consulate office of that country and ask for their commercial attache. In most situations, they will be able to give you at least some more specific information than you may already have. We have done this searching for some specialized combs in France and were given the names of five manufacturers in a very specific region where all inexpensive plastic items are made. Finding those sources without the assistance of the commercial attache would have taken considerably more effort, and in fact, we might not ever have found the direct factory source. Even if you do not know of a specific article you want, the commercial office can often direct you to an area where items of the general type within your interests originate.

This brings up another point. There is no reason why you, as an importer, should not expect to get wholesale prices for items if you can find their original source. However, a wholesale level simply does not exist in many countries. For example, in many places in the Middle East there is only one price. In fact, you often cannot get any quantity discount; if you buy one or forty thousand, the price is the same. Usually this occurs when the product is handmade and there is no added efficiency created by the additional production. However, often if you can discover a factory you can obtain a wholesale price, as a factory suggests a distribution system and, thus, a distribution markup. Generally you must prove to them that you are in fact a businessperson. In this situation there are sometimes quantity discounts. There are very few bargains left in Europe, but there is no reason why you cannot get a wholesale price from a factory for items which you feel are desirable and then sell them at a profit. The combs which we are looking at are for sale already in the United States, but we have a customer. He will buy them from us rather than from someone else as long as our price is not higher, and it shouldn't be, if we get a wholesale price from the factory or distributor.

Once you arrive in the country there are also numerous ways to locate goods which interest you. First, nearly every sizeable city will have a tourist office. If nothing else, you will probably find someone there who speaks your language and who can assist you in finding other organizations to assist you. Once on Oporto, Portugal, we were assisted greatly by the tourist office of the city. We could not speak Portuguese and wanted to find an export trade association in the telephone book. They did this for us, gave us the address and we made our contact.

Also, in nearly every city you will find a chamber of commerce. Their job usually is to connect people like yourself and organizations with goods to sell from their country. Once, when we were searching in Spain for a particular type of belt buckle which we had found here, we traveled the entire west coast of Spain in a car and stopped at all chambers of commerce asking whether this type of buckle was made in their city or region. Finally, we were lucky and were given a list of all factories and made a useful contact.

Another method is to attempt to contact all governmental agencies which are connected in any way with export. We did this in Casablanca. Upon seeing a building with the sword export on it, we entered and asked to speak with the director. We didn't get to see the director but were introduced to a wonderful man who proved helpful and whom we have enjoyed knowing. He put us in touch with the head of the apparel industry in Morocco who, in turn, connected us successfully with several manufacturers of the particular goods we were seeking.

Private trade associations for export are another type of organization which can be found in telephone books or through tourist offices. We found several on our travels, but particularly one in Portugal. We were seeking some firm or individual who could export the lovely handmade sweaters and socks of Portugal. We had searched all of northern Portugal and were continually told that it was impossible. In the end, a representative of a Portuguese trade association introduced us to a firm that was doing just that and in fact looking for someone in the United States to import their things.

There is another source of information and assistance which we have found useful. We might call them "export representatives." We developed a contact through the chamber of commerce in a small city in Spain with a group who acted as middlemen between exporters from Spain and importers to other countries. They handled all contacts and transactions and the prices which we paid were the same as if we had dealt directly with the factories (because the government subsidizes exporters and the amount saved is enough to pay the representative's fee). They often have samples of all items and you need only deal through them. They are responsible for quality control, timing, etc.

If you find something that you like and want to find out where it is made in the area, try asking a cabdriver to take you to the factory. The factory may not exist, but it doesn't hurt to ask and we have been successful with this method very often. Another offbeat method of finding the factory or source is to simply ask someone on the street and pay them to take you there. We did this once in Mexico where we found some shirts we loved. We stopped and asked a young Mexican if he knew where these shirts were made. He did, and took us to the factory where we purchased quite a few at a wholesale price. And even the owner of a store will sometimes help direct you to a wholesaler of items you may see and desire in larger quantities. It certainly doesn't hurt to ask.

Sometimes in order to get the best prices you must find the source and that takes a bit of creativity. But that can be fun. Some of our best contacts came that way. Never be afraid to ask! The worst anyone can say is no!

Now that you've decided you want it—you have to pay for it.

Chapter 7

THE GORY DETAILS

You've found a perfect inlaid box. You know it will sell in Des Moines, but how do you pay for it? How do you get it back to Des Moines? If your trip is exploratory, you'll probably just buy a couple of good, small samples at the best price you have been able to negotiate. You'll pack them in the extra empty suitcase you brought along, wrapped in dirty laundry and newspapers. However, regardless of size of purchase, you still have to pay for it. Sound simple? Maybe not!

≈ WHAT! YOU DON'T TAKE ≈ PERSONAL CHECKS!

You will probably pay with cash or utilize the traveler's checks you've brought along. The major world banks have advertised traveler's checks widely so most people are acquainted with and use them. For example, Bank of America or Citicorp traveler's checks, as well as those of American Express and Thomas Cook, are accepted fairly readily throughout the world. However, in many less developed countries, the merchants in the street market will not accept traveler's checks because they themselves have trouble cashing them in their banks. They will insist on cold, hard cash, most usually in the form of the currency of that country.

When dollar-denominated traveler's checks and dollars are accepted it will be at a rate of a certain quantity of the local currency for each dollar. It is important to watch this rate. With the current fluctuations of floating currencies, it can change daily. When you arrive in a country, study the exchange rates posted near the cashiers' windows at hotels and in various banks. Begin with the bank or "exchange" at the airport to start getting a feel for the rates. For example, you may find that you can get 200 yen for each dollar. But even if the so-called prevailing market rate is 195, you may get only about 180 yen for your dollar after paying for the exchange, depending on where you exchange. Further, upon departure you may find you have to pay 210 yen to buy a dollar. It is helpful to know, generally, what the rates of exchange are before you leave. This is not difficult, as most international banks such as Citicorp or Bank of America will be able to tell you what the current exchange rate is in the countries you will visit. You need only call the international department and inquire. These rates are also listed daily in most major newspapers in the business section under "foreign funds."

A bank will also be able to tell you how much of the currency of those countries you can buy in the United States with each dollar, assuming you are dealing with a country where the currency can be exchanged here. If the rate seems better at home and you are able to buy the currency (some currencies can only be purchased in the country of origin), it may be to your advantage to exchange some dollars in advance and arrive with foreign currency in hand.

We once arrived in Bali at four in the morning and found only a few policemen and taxi drivers around. The exchange window would not be open for another five hours. Because of currency restrictions the taxi drivers were reluctant even to take us to town with the prospect of dollar payments. Finally we convinced a driver that we could change our dollars for rupiahs at the hotel and he consented to take us. So, it usually is more convenient to have some currency of the country with you when you enter. We exchange some of our dollars at major international banks which regularly deal in foreign currency prior to our trip to places where the currency is available, thereby arriving with foreign currency in our pocket. Also, it might save you the "fee" sometimes charged by "changers" abroad.

On the other hand, in some countries you can get more local currency for your dollar than you can in the United States. In that case you want to defer purchasing most of the currency until you get there.

You will find that there is usually a difference between the exchange rate for currency and for traveler's checks. The amount of difference and whether it favors dollars or traveler's checks will depend on the demand for dollars in the particular country at the time. As a result, we always carry a fair sum of dollars with us so that we can take advantage of a situation when the actual greenback itself commands a premium rate. Obviously carrying currency rather than traveler's checks has risk of theft, which can be quite high in some regions of the world. So weigh that risk in your analysis.

Be sure to check on banking hours after you arrive. And be sure to pay the merchant, if possible, on a day when you are able to also exchange at a bank, in case he does the old "I can't get as much for your dollar today as I told you yesterday" routine. Your price goes up and so does his profit. Many countries, particularly in the Middle East, have much different business and banking hours than we do. Oftentimes, they are closed entirely on Fridays and open on Saturdays and Sundays. And, of course, they have different holidays, and in some countries more frequently—so learn the patterns of their culture so you don't get caught with only two more days in a place, both of which happen to be during an important festival when everything is closed.

Also, be very careful that you don't run afoul of foreign exchange controls. There are some countries where dollars can only be converted to local currency at authorized exchange dealers. Use of American dollars will be a violation of local law for both you and the merchant. You can find out whether there are any exchange restrictions by asking a bank or your hotel cashier. This information can also be obtained before you leave by calling the consulate or embassy of the country involved. Often in these countries you must retain cash conversion receipts and prove, upon exit from the country, that the dollars and total cost of merchandise leaving equals approximately the amount of money which you brought in and declared. Usually you are given these forms upon entering the country and return them when you exit. This is often found in countries where there are severe restrictions on taking local currency out of the country. If you try to leave with local currency, it may be confiscated with no compensation. If you are able to convert it back to dollars, this nearly always results in some financial loss. If after changing all your remaining rupiahs into dollars, you cannot prove that you used all of the rest of that currency obtained during your visit for purchases in some respect or another, you may be detained. We do personally know of one instance where a friend of ours spent several hours attempting to reconcile her purchases and exchange receipts (some of which she had thrown away) with several foreign customs officials. They threatened to confiscate her purchases *and* her remaining funds until she finally was able to convince them of her truthfulness.

And, beware of individuals approaching you on the street claiming to be legitimate money-changers who are often willing to pay substantial sums to obtain your dollars. In countries with currency restrictions, one often finds a black money market. If you deal with these people you could be in serious violation of local law.

Credit cards are not a reliable payment medium in the Importing Game. Often merchants of the sort you'll be dealing with will not accept them for several reasons. The most obvious is that they might not understand them or they may not have a banking relationship that allows them to accept credit cards. Even if they do, the merchant pays a substantial discount fee when converting them to cash. Additionally, they may be only usable at establishments where bargaining is not an acceptable practice. So you often do not get the best price, and we have never found them accepted in a wholesale buying situation.

Another risk with credit is that the exchange rate is not usually established until the charge slip is presented by the merchant to the credit card issuer's agent. Sometimes, if the exchange rate is volatile, the merchant may hold the charge slip for a while, hoping for a better rate. One method we have used to avoid this problem is to force the merchant to insert the U.S. dollar value on the charge slip.

Occasionally, although infrequently, a foreign merchant will accept a personal check on your own bank. This will usually only happen in places where there have been enough foreign visitors so the merchant has had experience with foreign checks and found no serious detriment to their use. We have also frequently found that the personal check is very readily accepted in situations where you are dealing with manufacturers or manufacturers' representatives at a wholesale level, particularly in Europe. Occasionally it has also occurred in some less-developed countries. Almost invariably a merchant who does accept a personal check does so only for goods which he is going to ship to you, and he will not commence shipment until he receives word from his bank that the check has cleared.

Of course, if your check is good, the merchant cooperative, and you intend to ship the goods anyway, a personal check can be a very convenient method of payment for both large and small shipments, *if* you trust the merchant. It can defer your actual payment by several weeks while the check clears, yet establishes an exact exchange rate for the goods at the moment the check is accepted by the merchant. Again, you will have to keep in mind the rate of exchange the merchant is using with regard to the dollars represented by your check.

Remember that the merchant probably is not going to ship the goods until the check clears. That may be a week or two, depending on the banking structure of the country and the intercountry clearing systems established between banks in that country and the U.S. Although we will say that in wholesale situations, both in the Middle East and in Europe, we are able to write personal checks *and* take the samples when we have presented ourselves as businesspeople (again, a business card helps!). In a couple of weeks you may already be home or in some other part of the world. Suppose the check clears and the merchant gets his money and he doesn't ship the goods. That is not an uncommon situation. It has caused many hours of concern for many people and is a difficult problem to solve.

Of course, if you were to pay cash you could have the same risk if the merchant were going to ship for you. However, there is not the check-clearing delay in this instance and you can often check back later that day or the following one to see if the shipment has been made.

Experiences with attempts to have items shipped are myriad. One English friend who purchases in Morocco for resale actually hires a truck, pays local workers to load the goods on the truck and rides the truck from Marrakech, Morocco, to Casablanca. She watches the goods being packaged and placed on the ship before she flies home. That friend has never had a shipping problem! However, not all of us have the time or inclination to go to such extremes.

There are reliable freight forwarders in many countries who often can be located through the American embassy, consulate or establishments such as the local American Express office. We once located one such company on a referral from the local American Express office in Afghanistan. We paid them $15 to pack the goods, clear them through customs and deliver them to the airport where they were shipped airfreight C.O.D.

to us in San Francisco. Everything arrived and it was well worth $15.

However, on another occasion we purchased items in Agadir, Morocco, paid the merchant to ship them, and did not receive them for over six months. Our letters were never answered and we did not happen to be in that part of the world in the interval. So we contacted the tourist and commercial offices in Morocco, which were branches of the government. We forwarded them our documents (remember to always receive proof of purchase, proof of payment and promise to ship) and our claim. They summoned the shopkeeper to their offices. We received the items within two weeks. We were fortunate. Do not count on such helpful intervention.

The problem of nonshipment is so hard to solve, in part because it is difficult to become sufficiently acquainted with a foreign merchant to know whether you can trust him until you have had a course of dealing with him. Because of this, the letter of credit has arisen as an important tool in international trade.

A documentary letter of credit is a promise by a bank to pay drafts (which are something like checks) which are drawn on the issuing (promising) bank and request the bank to pay the specified sums (if within the letter of credit's dollar limit) when the merchant, who signs the draft (the drawer), delivers it, together with required shipping documents (which prove the goods have been shipped), to the issuing bank's correspondent (local bank) in the merchant's country. As you can see, the letter of credit helps break the impasse which could inhibit trade between countries. The buyer does not pay until the goods have been shipped. But, the seller has the promise of a bank he knows that if the goods are shipped, he will get paid.

How do you get a letter of credit? You go to the international department of your bank, if it has one. If it doesn't, go to your banker and ask for his or her advice and recommendation to a bank which can provide the letter of credit and necessary international expertise. Since letters of credit can be a little difficult to understand, we have included as Appendix E excerpts from an excellent introduction to, and an explanation of, letters of credit. This will help dispel the mysteries of letters of credit and assist you in deciding whether they could be useful to you. As your business grows, an international banker can help you to finance your purchases through the use of time drafts and other forms of financing.

A letter of credit, however, is most workable in a situation where you know, before the letter is opened, precisely what you are buying.

It is quite usual, for instance, for the letter of credit to require a commercial invoice (which precisely describes what has been sold, its unit price and any other information, such as other costs, composition of goods, etc., which will be useful in clearing the goods through customs), consular invoices, the bill of lading (from the air or ocean carrier indicating that the goods have been put aboard the carrier for shipment), and the insurance certificate (which assures that you will be reimbursed if the goods are destroyed en route after you have paid for them).

It is important that you remember, however, that the bank is not a guarantor of the goods. It only has to assure that the documents presented are of the kind and content required. If the boxes shipped contain rags instead of goods it is of no concern of the bank as long as the documents recite that they contain whatever it was you wanted. Don't despair, however. The foreign merchant is usually too concerned with his own reputation to certify on an invoice and a packing list that he has shipped you inlaid ivory boxes when he has in fact shipped rags. It is not like his failing to ship things and being able to apologize for his "forgetfulness" or his "slowness." With the false invoice his duplicity is clear and so easily provable that it is less likely to happen.

Do make certain that you fill out the terms of the letter of credit completely. Your banker should be able to assist you regarding this and their experience may be helpful. Once we opened a letter of credit in which we thought we had carefully protected ourselves with explicit documentary requirements including a certificate that the goods be tagged with certain care instructions. The documents eventually submitted were as requested including the certificate on the care instructions. So the bank paid the seller as provided in the letter of credit. Finally the goods arrived and we found that as required they were tagged with the care instructions, but in French rather than English. This was unacceptable to United States Customs. We were stuck because we had not specified that the care instructions were to be in English.

If you don't know what you want to buy, but want the ability to assure payment of substantial sums as you discover things and they are shipped under your supervision, your international banker may be able to arrange a traveler's letter of credit for you. This usually requires establishing satisfactory credit with the issuing bank in advance but will allow you to obtain funds at local banks as needed up to the face amount of the credit.

As you see, in international trade transactions, your banker is an important friend. The facilities they can provide will make transactions considerably simpler and as the volume and sophistication of your trading grows, they will be able to suggest more sophisticated techniques to assist and protect you.

≈ THERE'S PACKING AND ≈ THERE'S PACKAGING

Once you've made your deal and arranged for payment, the practical problems of transportation arise. Before you even get too involved with how the goods are going to get back home, you have to resolve the problem of packing.

If you have only a few smaller things you can usually put them in a suitcase and bring them in yourself as part of your baggage. This involves no more than the common technique of trying to wrap the goods in clothing, isolated from the edges of the bag to protect them from any baggage-handling shocks.

When things get too large, voluminous or inappropriate for inclusion as baggage, packing becomes an issue. Why it is a concern becomes evident when you think about the abuse your suitcase gets in traveling. Then reflect for a moment, that is the most gentle treatment packages get in usual forms of transportation!

Airfreight, however, is usually handled much more carefully than ocean shipment. So if the weight, bulk and value of what you are shipping will justify airfreight movement, the extent of the packing required will be considerably reduced. Depending on the fragility of the goods, a light, strong cardboard box may be appropriate; just a good, protective package to preserve the surface of the object or to keep the articles together may be all that is needed.

The lesson to be kept in mind in airfreight movements is that you must try to find a reasonable balance between protection appropriate to the goods (keeping in mind the relatively gentle handling of airfreight) and the weight and hence transportation cost of the packaging material.

We once bought a lamp in Paris that we wanted in San Francisco in time for the Christmas season and told the seller that we wanted it packed and shipped airfreight. That was promised and we left Paris expecting the lamp momentarily. After several weeks, we wrote only to be assured that the lamp was being packed and would be here shortly. Two months later it arrived—after Christmas, of course—and it was only then that we realized our error. The seller was not familiar with foreign trade, being a local lamp manufacturer who did not produce for the export market. Confronted with an export situation, she did not want to take the risk of breakage. She had sent the lamp out to be given a usual packing by an export packing firm. The metal lamp, which weighed at most five pounds, arrived in an elegant wood packing crate which weighed fifty pounds. Since it was sent with the airfreight bill for our account, you can imagine our chagrin at not being sensitive to her lack of experience and specifying a more appropriate and lighter packaging.

Ocean transportation is more appropriate for heavier, lower value goods or those which are not excessively fragile. In earlier days, each box shipped by sea was loaded individually and was often thrown from hand to hand, into a net to be hoisted aboard. The boxes were then piled high in the ship's hold. This did not result in a very personalized attention for each box and export packing became a very routine practice of constructing strong wood boxes around the packages which were in transit.

The same basic rule applies even today, although the advent of the shipping container considerably reduced the amount of handling required for each package. If the goods are shipped by a freight forwarder who fills an entire container to your desired destination, the handling decreases significantly and the risks of breakage are reduced. Also, a sealed container is more difficult to loot, and pilferage, which was a common problem in precontainerized shipping days, is now minimized.

Still, as some of the goods with which your shipment travels are bigger and heavier, the handling is less personalized and there is a greater possibility of injury due to motion in carriage. So, packing for ocean transport should be significantly stronger, particularly so if the route of movement for your goods does not provide a through containerized service.

A related form of packing applies for material mailed. Even though it may seem an unusual way to bring in goods, it sometimes proves quite sensible if the goods aren't too heavy or bulky. This method is usually more expensive than airfreight per pound of article moved, but you have an added advantage of not being required to go through a generally more complex customs process over there. We have done this and it is not too difficult in most countries. You just go to the post office and fill out the proper forms and send it home airmail. This can be as simple as it sounds. In North Africa and the Middle East we have found particularly helpful assistance at post offices. One remarkable example occurred in Marrakech, Morocco, where a person had set up a booth at the post office and for a dollar or so would wrap your packages, fill out customs forms for you and assist in arranging for shipment with the local post office officials. While this was one unusually complete service, we have found that it is much less complicated to mail a package in foreign countries than we had originally imagined.

Keep in mind the condition of the last package you received from even two hundred miles away through the mail and that will guide you as to how well to pack your things for parcel post or airmail. You need be concerned that this package will possibly spend three weeks in transit, being thrown around many times, and with the possibility of weather damage to the item and packaging. Failure to pack and wrap parcels adequately is a major source of parcel damage. It's to your benefit to prepare parcels to withstand weather, heedless handling, vibration and the weight of other packages. Also be sure the address is legible. Don't use felt tip markers or other washable inks that smear in the rain! Be sure the address label is securely attached. You should place address information inside the package too, in the event the outside address label is lost or obliterated. We also suggest some sort of plastic covering on the item to protect against water damage.

We have sent and received many successful parcel post shipments, however, two disasters stand out in our minds. One was a leather purse we sent ourselves from Italy. When it arrived many weeks later, it remained only as a box of mold—water damage. Another occasion found us with the remains of some Australian wine—broken bottles and a red stain on the box—improper packaging.

≈ WHAT'S THE CHEAPEST WAY ≈ TO GET THIS BACK FROM OVER THERE?

Now that it's packed and paid for, let's get it home. As we said earlier, airfreight has many advantages for moving cargo if the goods are of the proper sort. Airfreight rates are generally higher (per pound) than ocean freight rates and are based on a combination of weight, value and bulk. The reason airfreight rates are based on weight is obvious. A plane can only lift so many thousand pounds and maximum revenue must be obtained for each pound if the venture is to be profitable. Volume is related. If a large inflated balloon were carried, the plane's revenue weight basis would be minimal since the space taken by the balloon would eliminate the possibility for other revenue-producing cargo. So, by air you basically want a light, small commodity with packaging as light as is reasonably necessary to protect the goods in order to obtain the best rate.

There are different commodity rate bases. This is because some goods such as perishable commodities can only be sent by air. Another sort are goods of a high value such that increased time for ocean carriage will cost the owner more in interest or lost use of capital than the airfreight rate. Fine jewelry or electronic components may be examples. Other goods require speed for their value; emergency parts and high-fashion clothing are such. Sometimes, a particular commodity may be cheaper or more expensive by air than the weight and bulk would suggest. Acquaintance with the tariff schedules of the various carriers will be important as they are complicated. A freight forwarder or other transportation specialist may be helpful. There is some value in checking out airfreight rates prior to your departure so you can figure in this cost generally at the time of purchase to attempt to determine the real cost (cost of item, freight cost plus customs duty). You need only call the freight department of any major international airline to obtain this information. They usually have very up-to-date rate schedules and are glad to help you. Just keep in mind that this information is not necessarily an exact rate.

If you are trying to obtain an airfreight rate abroad, beware of incorrect information. Often the seller or other freight forwarder will call the airlines and obtain a rate per kilo from them. We have found ourselves quoted a freight rate in dollars which they created by using an arbitrary classification, an invalid exchange rate, and finally adding a percentage on for the seller or others without saying so. If you know the freight rate in the foreign currency, you can supply the appropriate exchange rate and eliminate any surprises.

Assuming it seems clear that the goods you want to move should go by air, then the transportation phase is generally rather easy. Aircraft (whether cargo aircraft or regular passenger aircraft which often have significant air cargo capacity) go regularly to most places these days. Most airlines belong to the International Air Transportation Association (IATA) and follow comparable procedures and standards. Even though the trip may require the use of several air carriers, the movement will usually be done in one single continuous air bill from origin to destination, thereby allowing you to trace the shipment from place to place. We have on occasion lost a shipment for a week or so. Having the air waybill in our possession helped immensely in locating this lost shipment as an air waybill number is easily traceable and the air waybill usually states the routing, i.e., Shanghai, Hong Kong, Tokyo, Honolulu, Los Angeles, San Francisco.

Ocean freight is often more variable, the service often less predictable, and possibly not available at your point of purchase. That massive wood carving you found in Nuristan, which is too heavy to reasonably go by air, will probably have to be heavily crated, trucked thousands of miles through Afghanistan and portions of the old U.S.S.R. (because there are no railroad lines) to a port on the Black Sea or in Lebanon, Turkey or Germany. There it will be off-loaded in the port, await an appropriate ship, and, if there is no direct ocean service to your specified port of entry, it will have to be off-loaded and reloaded at some intermediate port to another vessel which calls at your desired destination. You can see that the complexity of the movement, the possible delay, and the risk of loss or injury (ranging from someone forgetting about it in a corner of a warehouse in Iskenderun to destruction in a truck accident or bandit raid) is significant. Some acquaintances were in fact bringing some of their Nuristan carvings back and had them loaded aboard a truck. The truck had reached the Afghan-Iran border at the time of the 1978 coup in Afghanistan. All governmental functions stopped for about a week while the bureaucrats tried to decide what policies, if any, were now applicable. During that week, our acquaintances sat on the top of the truck at the customs post on the border. Finally, the officials concluded that there had been no changes in export policy and the truck was allowed to proceed through the checkpoint and out of the country.

Of course, for smaller items parcel post is a possibility. For small packages which you want quickly and without a fuss, parcel post can be a reasonable alternative, particularly because a minimum service charge is added to send items by air- or ocean freight when the number of kilos is small. You pay for this amount whether your shipment is less or not. It may actually be cheaper to send it airmail, and as mentioned earlier, often the outgoing customs procedures are much easier.

Routing of shipments and choices between competing carriers are complex issues about which it is difficult to generalize. It is a subject on which expert guidance should be sought until you are well acquainted with the factors involved and even then your freight forwarder will still be your best friend.

≈ WHAT DO YOU MEAN I CAN'T ≈ TAKE IT OUT OF THE COUNTRY?

Could it really happen? You've bought something, paid for it, and wrapped it safely in clothing in the middle of your suitcase. Several days later you are leaving the country, hundreds of miles from the place where you bought it. The airport procedure requires opening your bags—probably searching for drugs or contraband. Your turn comes and the customs agent feels around in your bag and all of a sudden seems to have found something. You are stunned. He pulls out that lovely little figurine, says "no" and takes it away into an office while you look on in bewilderment.

You have just had a very sad lesson in the fact that many countries try to preserve their cultural heritage by prohibiting the export of important cultural assets, and more importantly, that it is up to you to find out their prohibitions because often the merchant is only interested in making a sale and cares little whether or not you can, in fact, take the article out of the country. Sometimes the merchant will sell the information that you are carrying such goods to someone else who gives the tip-off. And, of course, you do not get reimbursed for the item. It is confiscated.

How do you avoid this unfortunate experience? By inquiry concerning export restrictions. Once you know about them, they can often be taken care of through certain governmental agencies and museum clearances before you make your purchase. The merchant can sometimes expedite this for you if you make it clear the sale is contingent on his successful assistance in obtaining needed documents.

We have obtained museum clearances in many places with little or no trouble. One occasion in Costa Rica stands out in our minds, however. We attempted to get one for some pre-Columbian artifacts we had purchased even though the seller insisted that this clearance was not needed. We felt certain it was, as we had checked before we made the trip. So, we personally obtained one and were glad that we did, as we were required to show our documents at the border in order to avoid confiscation of our purchases.

In Appendix A we list the American consulates and/or embassies throughout the world whom you can contact, before you buy, for further information about prohibited or restricted items.

Well, you finally got it out—now, how do you get it in? Don't panic; customs really can be fun—well, maybe not fun—but at least interesting.

Chapter 8

CUSTOMS? OH NO!

Customs! You probably know about customs from the viewpoint of a returning tourist. As an importer you deal with the same people and the same law, but from a different point of view. However, it really is not as bad as it's made out to be if you approach it with a positive attitude and are somewhat forewarned. Here are a few guidelines which should help you. Keep in mind, however, that Customs law is in constant change. As you know from the daily news, trade is a significant aspect of the world economy and trade imbalances cause continuing political effects. One of those effects is reflected in tinkering with the laws administered by the Customs Service. While the general trend over the past decades is toward liberalization of trade through reduction of tariffs and some restraints on trade, there has, at the same time, been an increase in other types of restraints such as quotas. Trade-sensitive items is our term for those products which are of concern in trade negotiations, such as cotton textiles.

Because of this frequent adjustment, the traditional Tariff Schedule of the United States (commonly known as TSUS) which appeared as part of the Customs law was repealed in 1988. It was replaced by the Harmonized Tariff Schedule (now known as HTSUS), which sought to more completely coordinate the U.S. classification system with the systems of our worldwide trading partners. One consequence of this is that the Tariff Schedule is now maintained and published by the U.S. International Trade Commission. A copy of the current text is available for purchase through the Superintendent of Documents, U.S. Government Printing Office, Washington, D.C. 20401. Since the law and regulations are in a state of flux, you should always check with Customs or your customhouse broker for exact details.

Remember the time you drove back in from a trip to Canada or Mexico and were asked if you had bought anything there? Depending upon your answer, you were either passed, were asked to show the articles you purchased, or had your car thoroughly inspected. It was easy, right? And not too time consuming.

If you come in from abroad on an airplane, you receive a small card on which you are asked to list all of your purchases abroad and what you paid for them. This is the Customs declaration. Always fill it out completely and accurately.

Presume that you bought goods which cost you approximately $500 while on your trip. A returning United States resident who has been abroad for more than a couple of days has the right to bring in merchandise with a value of $400 U.S. free of duty (and an additional $400 for goods acquired in American Samoa, Guam and the U.S. Virgin Islands), but this is only on items for personal use. Under provisions designed to foster economies of countries in the Caribbean Basin, the exemption is increased to $600 for goods from that region.

When you declare commercial items (items for resale) you are not able to use your traveler's exemption, but you will not pay substantially more duty on an item than you would have if it had been purchased for personal use. The difference is that application of the tariff rate schedules of duty have been dropped in favor of a flat ten percent rate on the value, in excess of the exemption, of articles for noncommercial purposes which accompany a returning U.S. resident, up to $400.

Since tariff rates are both higher and lower than ten percent, whether the application of the ten percent flat rate would be beneficial or detrimental will depend on the tariff rates applicable to the particular goods imported. Appendix H provides two examples of the computation provided by the Customs Service which may help explain this calculation.

During the customs process many are tempted to "forget" to mention some items or to undervalue others. That is not smart. You should have purchased each article at a price far below that which it would have cost in the United States. Most likely this will still be the case after duty has been paid. If you are purchasing for resale, this is a cost which is simply passed on to the purchaser of your goods. The merchandise should still be marketable here since anyone else bringing in the same type of item also will have to add a similar duty to their costs. Customs duty is simply an added cost of doing business, and one which is directly recoverable upon resale of the merchandise.

You will not be required to stand in any separate line because you have declared articles for resale. You need only state "for resale" on your Customs declaration and list each item and its price. When you reach customs, the first thing you are usually asked is where you have been on your trip and that is compared with the entry on your Customs declaration. In asking that question the customs agent is ascertaining the possible place of purchase and evaluating the merchandise and its cost against their experience covering prices in those areas and the general provisions of the customs law. The customs agent may then look through your bags and examine some of the items. They may look at some of the items more closely, write a number down on the card and perhaps refer to their black book. They may say, "Okay, you can go."

To understand what the customs agent is doing is important, both for a better awareness of what is going on when you go through customs yourself, and also to know what to expect when you attempt to clear goods through customs on an unaccompanied entry. Let's look a bit more closely at the customs law. There are several ways in which customs classifies import movement. Certain imports are classified as informal entries. Household and personal effects of returning U.S. residents not imported under a purchase agreement and not intended for sale may be entered informally without a dollar limit, when contained in a passenger's baggage. This provision allows the traveler to bring back articles for personal use under informal entry procedures.

Broadly speaking you can informally enter a fairly substantial value of goods with your baggage provided such goods are not intended for sale. So long as the trade-sensitive items which accompany you are worth less that $250, you are entitled to informally enter up to $1,250 of accompanying goods for resale. You may be able to enter a greater value of goods for resale if the value in excess of $1,250 is represented by a commercial invoice and the informal entry is not burdensome on the customs officer.

The provisions allowing for such informal entry of personal goods provides that it applies when the "... arriving person is carrying a few dutiable or taxable articles which can be readily identified and segregated from articles entitled to free entry under [the person's] personal exemptions . . . ." 19 C.F.R. §148.12 (b) (1) (i). So the customs officer has a fair amount of discretion in allowing an informal entry under a baggage declaration. A word to the wise is to make the process easy and pleasant for the customs officer.

Thus, under certain conditions you may also include in accompanying baggage informal entry goods which are intended for sale. In mid-1992 you were entitled to do so if the total value of such goods was less than $1,250 and the value of trade-sensitive items was less than $250 in value. In mid-1992, those trade-sensitive items included plastics and rubber articles (Section VII of the HTSUS); raw hides, furs, articles of leather (Section VIII); textiles and textile articles (Section XI); footwear (Section XII); furniture, bedding and lamps (Chapter 94);

and articles subject to quotas and other modifications under trade legislation and the Agricultural Adjustment Act (Chapter 99, Subchapters III and IV). You also could bring in a greater value of nontrade goods for sale if you provided a commercial invoice and the customs officer determined that the entry was not burdensome.

Of course you don't intend to sell your samples, so you can easily bring them back with you to enable you to test the market.

So, if your entry is relatively easy for the customs officer and does not include an excessive value of trade-sensitive goods, you may be able to achieve an informal entry of goods you intend to sell with your baggage as you return home.

Let's say that you have found lots of merchandise and there's more than you can reasonably include in your baggage. One frequently used alternative is mail or parcel post. Since these items do not accompany you they will not be included in your customs exemption. Thus they will be subject to duty when they arrive in the U.S. The post office sends all mail shipments received from abroad to the Customs Service for examination. The Customs Service will examine the declaration attached to the package. If the goods are not dutiable, the package will be released for delivery without further fees.

If the declaration attached to the packaging indicates dutiable items and if formal entry is not required due to the trade-sensitive nature of the goods, the Customs Service will attach a mail entry to the package. This will specify the amount of duty due. The package with the mail entry will be returned to the post office. On delivery the postal service will collect the duty together with a nominal Customs Service processing fee on the dutiable packages. Many people have found the mail entry to be the easiest, most cost-efficient method of importing small quantities of commercial goods.

Once you get the big order, then you might well want to ask your contact abroad to ship it to you. When that shipment arrives it will not be part of your baggage. This will be an unaccompanied arrival, nonmail entry—what is called a "formal" entry. You may accomplish a formal entry but you will generally find it more efficient and economical to have a customhouse broker clear the shipment for you.

When the goods arrive, U.S. Customs will hold them at the point of entry and you will be required either to appear personally or to hire a customs broker to enter the goods. We will discuss this process in detail shortly. Usually you will use what is called a "consumption entry," which means the goods are going to be used in the United States.

Goods are legally imported when 1) they have arrived at a port of entry, 2) when forms appropriate to the particular type of entry have been presented to customs by the person who is to receive the goods (the consignee), and 3) any applicable duty has been paid. When you have submitted the required forms and documents, you have made an "entry."

Since you are entitled to make an informal entry, let's walk through an informal consumption entry arriving by ship or air to learn how it works.

You've received notice from the steamship company or the airline that your goods will be arriving next Tuesday. The notice says that you must pay a handling fee of $5 and indicates that the goods must be picked up at a specified warehouse in five days to avoid demurrage. Don't panic! It's not really that complicated.

The goods are on a plane or ship which has arrived at the port of entry closest to your home. The plane or ship is unloaded and the contents which are not immediately claimed (such as perishable or very high priority cargo) are placed in a warehouse to await pickup by the owners or owners' agents. The carrier places a time limit on pickup because it's not in the warehouse business. If you leave the merchandise there beyond the free period, you pay a storage fee called "demurrage."

But while the goods have arrived in the country, they haven't been "entered" for customs purposes. So, not only must you pick up the goods from the carrier within the time limit, but you must also clear them through customs so that they are legally entered goods.

You go to the warehouse of the shipping company from which you received your notice of arrival and to which you have been directed after payment of the fee. You present your notice form together with the original consignee's copy of the bill of lading. The clerk examines the bill of lading to assure that all freight charges have been paid since the carrier has a lien against the goods for the freight charges. That right is lost once the goods are released to the consignee. That's why the clerk is always careful to check the bill of lading before release and collect any payment due.

Then you are directed to the warehouse floor where a warehouseman will assist you in locating the goods and delivering them, in their packing box, to the customs official at the warehouse. This is like coming up to the customs officer when you arrive at an airport.

You again present yourself with the imported goods, still in their import packaging, for an entry. You hand the customs officer the bill of lading and an invoice which describes the goods in general and their cost to you, and you will be asked where you got them.

What does the customs officer do then? Two very important analytic steps which, while not evident in every entry, are nevertheless done. The customs officer 1) ascertains dutiable value and 2) classifies the goods according to certain statutory classifications.

≈ VALUATION ≈

Generally, customs officers have considerable experience with goods of the type they are evaluating and may know their value better than you do. Therefore, the values that they ultimately determine are legally presumed to be correct unless you can prove that some other value is correct. Generally, the price agreed upon between buyer and seller in arm's-length negotiations is the best indication of value and may not be rejected by Customs except in specific circumstances. This is one reason why it can be very important to have obtained an invoice at the time you purchased the goods.

Keep in mind that the dutiable value of the goods is not necessarily the price you paid abroad nor is it the retail value in the United States. Essentially, the officer is trying to set "transaction value" which is most usually "export value." Both of these terms are defined by statute.

Transaction value would generally be the purchase price of the goods plus amounts for certain other items if they are not included in the price. These items include:

1. Packing costs incurred by the buyer
2. Selling commission incurred by the buyer
3. The apportioned value of any "assist" (an example of an assist is the value of a pattern provided by the U.S. buyer to the foreign seller to enable the manufacture for the U.S. buyer)
4. Any royalty or license fee payable by buyer as a condition of the sale
5. Proceeds due to the seller for any subsequent resale or use of the imported goods

The cost of international freight and insurance may be deducted from the transaction cost if the price of the goods included insurance and freight to the U.S. entry destination.

The transaction value may not be used if the buyer and seller are related unless the Customs Service determines that the transaction value closely approximates the transaction value of identical or similar merchandise in unrelated sale. The Customs regulations provide other methods of valuation if the transaction price is suspected by the Customs Service due to the relationship of the parties or other causes.

≈ CLASSIFICATION ≈

Rates of duty are set out in the Harmonized Tariff Schedule of the United States. This schedule specifies a particular rate or group of rates for each classification of goods.

The Harmonized Commodity Description and Coding System, which is at the base of the HTSUS, was developed by the international trade community in the 1970s and 1980s in an effort to develop a uniform system of commodity description and coding which would be applicable in many countries. It was hoped that uniformity would provide greater consistency of tariff application as well as a basis for increased use of electronic data processing for trade movements.

Without getting into the explanation of the differences, it is generally thought that the HTSUS is conceptually simpler than the classification system found in the Tariff Act of 1930. That is certainly a benefit to the average importer.

Rates in the HTSUS, as under previous laws, vary between classifications, so precise classification can have important consequences.

HTSUS attempts to describe goods with great precision. However, despite hundreds of provisions, much room for disagreement exists because an article can arguably be covered by more than one description. Also, new products not described and new uses of old products or materials may, of course, create ambiguity.

Determinations involving classification disagreements are made by the Customs Courts. The issues often seem petty but the economic effects can be quite important. For instance, under the old tariff schedules, the Customs Court had to decide whether a mechanical singing bird in a brass cage was classifiable as a musical instrument. Was an electric toothbrush a toothbrush? In both cases, the court said "yes." On the other hand, an umbrella made of cloth but designed to put over food to protect it from insects was not an umbrella for tariff purposes.

Sample pages from the Harmonized Tariff Schedule of the U.S. (HTSUS) are shown in Appendix G to give you an idea of how it works.

You will note that there are two columns with different rates in the tariff schedule after each classification. The first column is subdivided into General and Special categories. The applicable rate will depend upon the country of origin (that is, place of manufacture, not place of purchase) of the goods. Generally, the higher tariff rate (column 2) is applicable for goods from certain countries which are in disfavor with the United States. This category was initially the countries that used to be called the Communist bloc. Its composition is changing rapidly.

Certain goods from developing countries in special groups are exempted from the usual duty or subject to a reduced rate of duty. These special duty classifications are summarized under the Special category of column 1. They include the special treatment for countries eligible under the Generalized System of Preferences (GSP). Goods manufactured in those countries are entitled to duty-free entry. A review of that column of the HTSUS is a guide to certain products for which duty-free treatment may be accorded. Also included in the Special category are other forms of special duty treatment such as is provided under the U.S.-Canada Free Trade. Included in Appendix B is a list of specially treated countries as of the 1992 HTSUS. Since details vary, it is important to check with Customs with regard to the special status of any specific article from a particular source. This can be a significant competitive advantage if you can discover goods which are made in a specially treated country and not otherwise excluded from the list because of the trade-sensitive nature of the product. You could avoid all duty on those items.

You will also note from the sample pages of the HTSUS in Appendix G that most duties are a percentage of value. This means that the duty is the indicated percentage of the ascertained transaction value which we discussed earlier. However, other duties are not related to value, but are assessed in relation to weight or on a per item basis without regard to value.

Because of the complexity of classification, it is not usually possible for the occasional importer to have a useful comprehension of the classification issues involved in importations. The Customs Service is aware of this, which is why they classify informal entries without detailed explanation but require the importer to provide classifications for formal entries.

It can be beneficial to try to ascertain the applicable duty for certain items you know you will want to purchase. For example, if you've brought back a sample which seems to have a potential market, you will want to show the items to a Customs representative to ascertain its commercial dutiable role before you set your prices. If we are looking for a certain kind of product, we try to check with Customs before we go so that, upon our return, we will know if an error is being made in some quick determinations that are often made at the airport. You can do this by telephoning your customs office and asking for the commercial rates department. Describe the item in detail. They cannot always tell you what the duty will be without seeing a sample but should be able to give you a general idea. For these and other reasons, the importer uses a customhouse broker in most formal entries.

Knowledge of customs duties can also be valuable on your noncommercial trips or with regard to items brought back for your personal use. If you know the items imported for personal use which are subject to the highest duty, you can list those items first on your Customs declaration. That will enable your exemptions to be applied against the products bearing the highest duty, leaving the low-duty items as those not covered by the exemption.

Once the type and origin of the goods has been established, the customs officer may wish to examine the goods to verify that the initially anticipated classification is correct and that the value is as represented. Do not be tempted by the foreign seller who offers to provide you with a reduced price invoice "to help you with customs." Double or false invoicing is often discovered because the customs officer is often better acquainted with the value of certain goods than you are. And it can be extremely embarrassing, at best, to be caught. The risks aren't worth it!

An interesting example of how sensitive the customs officers are to values was shown in an instance when we brought in a Japanese screen on which there was a hand-painted scene. The screen was quite large but because the painting was old and of a nontraditional subject, it had not been popular in Japan. We therefore had purchased it at a very low price. When the customs officer asked about the shipment, we told him it was an original painting mounted on a screen. We thus anticipated that it would be classified as an original work of art enterable without duty. On the other hand, a screen (a piece of furniture with decoration thereon) would be dutiable. He made us uncrate it and examined the painted surface very carefully to see that it was in fact an original work of art that had been mounted on a screen. When he discovered the artist's signature in the corner, he cleared it for entry without duty.

By the way, when you uncrate imports at customs, it is up to you to get rid of the debris yourself. This can be quite a chore. Often the warehousemen will do it for you if you give them something to cover their costs in disposing of the material.

When the goods arrive, if the value is low enough and the volume or bulk is slight, go pick it up yourself. It can be an adventure and add to your knowledge as an importer. But for any substantial shipments, see a good customhouse broker. Their services can probably save you substantial fees by assuring appropriate customs classification and valuation.

A customs broker has the necessary bonding and expertise to handle formal entries into the Untied States. They can usually be found listed in the yellow pages of the telephone book under Customhouse Brokers. Or, sometimes, someone at the U.S. Customs Service will suggest some names to you.

The broker fills out all forms necessary to have the shipment entered into the U.S. You will have to sign a power of attorney authorizing the broker to act on your behalf. The broker will need an invoice and bill of lading or airway bill for the shipment in order to fill out the forms necessary for the customs agent. This will take care of preliminary assignment of duty and if samples are requested by a customs agent (yes, that can happen too!), will take care of providing them. We believe customs brokers are well worth their very nominal fee.

Once the shipment has been entered the broker will, at your request, arrange drayage or make arrangements for you to pick up the items at the airline or wherever they are being held. You will have to pay the broker's fee, expenses, and duty at or before the time you receive the items.

Okay, the shipment has arrived and actually been entered into the United States. Are you in business? Not unless you sell it. Sell! Did you forget about that?

Chapter 9

TAKE YOUR MONEY AND RUN—BACK ABROAD

You are on a plane, daydreaming on your return flight from Nepal. Your suitcase is filled with potentially salable treasures. If you sell them your trip will be paid for. Then you remember that you've never sold anything in your life since the fourth-grade school magazine drive. Don't panic. Your first sale may be to the friend picking you up at the airport, who, seeing the lovely antique coat you are wearing, wants one immediately. How convenient that you just happen to have one in your luggage and offer it to her, for a price above your cost and considerably below the cost in a retail store. That was easy. She was a friend. Now she is also a customer.

Or the first day at your office you may wear that lovely amber necklace you purchased, to the envy of your coworkers. How convenient, you liked it so much, you purchased several which are similar. Of course, you'd be willing to sell them to your fellow employees. That, too, was easy. You were dealing with friends—but they are also now customers and helping you pay for your next trip!

We have made many sales to friends, friends of friends, and friends of friends of friends. Dealing with friends is a pleasant and easy way to begin to learn to sell. Returning after a major trip, Mary wore a beautiful peasant dress while lunching with a friend. The friend wanted one. We had liked them so much we had purchased several. We sold her one over lunch. She purchased a dress for considerably less than the retail store price. We had both profited considerably. She was still a friend, but she was helping us to develop our market.

Your friends can be the first market test of your new items. Remember the friends who always compliment you on your taste. Invite them over to see the slides of your trip, but make sure you use the opportunity to show them more than slides. Bring your purchases to their attention either by wearing them, displaying them, or using them. Or just bring them out and show them as remembrances of the country you have visited. If someone comments on liking one enough to own it, tell them you bought a couple extra which you are planning to sell. One of your guests may well be one of your first customers.

Our friends are especially interested in seeing our antique jewelry collection. Dinner party conversation tends to lead toward an inspection. We have made a number of sales just this way. Friends are usually very excited about a new venture and will want to see what treasures you have. We feel certain that there will be no complaints. Also, at this point, your friends may know of someone else who would be interested in the type of things you are bringing back—another potential customer!

One of our friends purchased some embroidered clothing from us. We made $75 on the sale. However, the benefit continued because she referred us to a friend of hers who owned a small import boutique. The owner of the store has since become a valued customer and we have earned hundreds of dollars from her purchases. We found it easier initially to approach a store buyer if we could say, "So and so suggested that I call."

Or what about that acquaintance of yours who owns a store or is a buyer for a store? Stores are constantly looking for merchandise to sell, and distinctive merchandise is much in demand. The owner of an antique shop not only purchased several pieces of jewelry from us, but referred us to numerous friends of hers. She also referred us to sources of unusual items in foreign countries, providing many more profitable trips and expanding our sources of goods abroad. Soon you will find yourself developing a large group of potential customers, all of whom are excited to see your things. As your reputation grows, chances are they will start calling you to find out whether you have any new and wonderful things for them to buy!

What about those shopkeepers or salespersons at the boutique near your home that you frequent? Have you developed friendships with any of them? If you wear some of your more interesting things, they may notice them and ask you about them. We have found this to be a particularly effective method, especially for an unusual piece of jewelry which will nearly always draw attention. Even if you are trying to sell baskets, the jewelry may provide an opening. Or, if you feel bold, ask them if you may bring some in to show them. We were once in a small store near our office after returning from a trip. While waiting to meet with the buyer, we overheard a conversation going on with another seller. This young woman had entered the shop earlier in the day wearing something quite extraordinary. Its beauty caused the salespeople to comment and query her as to its origin. It was an import by the young woman's small import company. They asked her to return with samples. She did and made a very substantial sale.

Your friends in the retail business will have other friends in the retail business. Once a friend who owned a small boutique could not use our items, but graciously referred us to another boutique down the street. She felt that the other store had our "look" while hers did not. We sold $270 worth of our merchandise in five minutes and, more importantly, developed a continuing business relationship with this second store. That contact in turn led us to other stores with personal introductions and helped us make substantial profits.

Many small museums have shops attached to them with items of sale from all over the world. You may be able to interest them in some of your purchases. The people working there most frequently are easy to approach as they are often there in a volunteer capacity. We find such people often have a real interest in the store and its merchandise.

United Nations (UNICEF) Centers are found in many U.S. cities. They generally have a gift shop and are constantly on the lookout for "imports" to improve the quality of their stock. The employees "volunteer" status again makes them pleasantly approachable.

If you are fearless, take a booth at a local flea market. We have a friend who did and who was grossing $500 a weekend. It's been done by other people we know and substantial benefits obtained. Go to the local flea market and inquire as to how you go about obtaining a booth. A word of caution—if you do take a booth and also sell to retail stores locally, you should take care not to compete in price with them on identical items. In other words, you should sell at the same price that your retail stores have to sell those items at in their stores. If you sold to them at a profit and then turned around and sold for less than they are able, to their potential customers, they may understandably become very angry.

Put an ad in the newspaper. Advertise goods of a certain nature from a certain area of the world. We have a friend who lived for a substantial period of time on the profits of $10,000 to $20,000 per year derived solely by this method. Another business friend also advertised, and while he only made several hundred dollars from it, his profit still made it worthwhile for him. Just be a bit cautious. If you have your items at your home and they are valuable, you will want to carefully screen anyone coming in. Additionally, you should check with local and state officials to see whether you need any type of permit to operate in this manner. In some states if you sell to anyone you need either to retain their resale number or, if they do not have one, to charge sales tax for the state. While we do not feel the need to get into this extensively, it is something you should be aware of.

Ads in magazines are also a possibility. Our own experience, however, has been that they are very expensive and provide you more with a mailing list of people interested rather than substantial profits. But be sure you inquire about the laws involved in offering items for sale under this method. Usually your local post office can help you.

Another enjoyable method of selling is to give one or more large parties each year solely for the purpose of displaying and hopefully selling your treasures. We know of someone who has done this, quite successfully, with her imports from Italy. Her friends enjoy a great party and the opportunity to purchase some unusual items for very reasonable prices. Our friend enjoys a great party and makes some money for her next trip.

You may try to obtain a booth at a gift or other related wholesale trade show. Contact the trade show association in your city for information. These people may be found by looking up "gift show" preceded by the name of your city, such as "San Francisco Gift Show." They will generally be very helpful in assisting you to obtain a booth to display your goods at shows. They also generally have information about shows in other cities throughout the United States. One company we know of, which is now very successful, started just this way. Two partners who were interested in importing and traveling came back from a trip with items and took a booth at the local gift show without knowing for sure whether they would even be able to obtain items if anyone ordered them. They were tremendously successful and filled their orders by taking another trip. Currently, they have a large wholesale business, a retail store, and lots of travel experience. We have tried both gift and boutique shops and have had fair success. You do not necessarily need to have reorder business to be a participant. In the Chicago Gift Show one successful importer filled her booth with one-of-a-kind articles from her travels and was very successful in not only making a substantial profit over the cost of her trip, but developed some fine new customers.

If you are unable to find a buyer, you may wish to put your items in a shop on consignment. This means that you leave your merchandise at a store to be sold. The store does not purchase the item outright (you still own it), but will offer it for sale to their numerous customers. You will receive money only if it sells in an amount previously agreed upon by you and the store. Many smaller stores often agree to this method. It allows them interesting merchandise with no capital outlay. You must decide what price you want for the item. The store then will generally sell it for at least double that amount, the difference being their profit. Be sure to make arrangements concerning how long an item will be in the store, when you will get your money, and when you will pick up unsold items. You should also have an understanding concerning damage or loss.

We have placed articles on consignment several times when we have had difficulty selling them otherwise. This way the store has no money at stake in the merchandise and it gives you a chance to recoup money laid out for an unwise purchase or samples you no longer need. While our greatest profits have not come this way, our initial investment in many items has been recovered.

We have on occasion approached the large chain stores. They are as anxious as smaller stores to obtain unusual merchandise. However, while they often buy more of an item, they generally buy more "common" looking things, that is to say, they are generally less daring in their buying. You can call and make an appointment to see a particular buyer or simply show up and ask for her time. Most buyers seem to prefer that one call first and make an appointment. If your item sounds interesting enough, they will more than likely see you. But be persistent. Rarely it seems will buyers actually return your call. They simply have no time. Vendors are constantly vying for their time and they are usually quite busy. So keep on calling and eventually you'll probably connect.

We had numerous rejections before landing a $4,200 sale. The buyer was so impressed with our item that she referred us to two sister stores. We called on them the same day and landed sales in excess of $3,300. She then referred us to her buying conglomerate in the East who referred us to all other affiliated stores. The result was thousands of dollars more in profitable sales. It all started with one easy phone call. That phone call which seems so difficult and frightening to make is really easy—the worst they can say is no. And even if they say no—try again in a couple of weeks—their buying situation may have changed or there may be a new buyer who is interested.

On another occasion, we simply walked into one of the poshest stores headquartered in our city and asked to see the buyer. We were somewhat surprised the buyer did see us, immediately. Later she told us that they would see anyone who walked in the door with an item, as some of their best goods came to them that way. We had some sample silk shawls to sell. We made a very large sale in less than thirty minutes and had to return to the country of origin to assure that we could deliver!

But you need not have hundreds of a product to sell to larger stores; often they will purchase only half a dozen to several dozen of an unusual item to offer as a treat to their customers and to make their own store more interesting. We have sold as few as six to such stores. Oftentimes it seems as though they actually prefer the smaller amounts as it assures them the product will not be seen everywhere else and they truly have a unique item.

You may wish to expand your market by finding a sales representative. We found our representative by choosing a store with merchandise similar to ours and of a quality we respected. We asked the saleswoman and ultimately the owner who sold them these items. With this information we were able to contact him. This established sales rep had a lot of things that we lacked: credibility among buyers, a multitude of contacts, a fine ability to sell, and booths at all the regular gift and boutique shows. We discovered that people who would not order from us previously would do so if "Harry" handled our line. They know he screened the people he represented and that he would be responsible for delivery. Buyers do not want to tie up their money for weeks without being assured of delivery. People who ordered our merchandise and demanded delivery within a week were willing to wait up to ninety days when Harry wrote the order. People who were willing to try only small amounts from us invariably wrote larger orders through Harry.

The cost is usually minimal, somewhere around ten to fifteen percent of the wholesale cost. But here again, you need not necessarily have a potentially large reorder business in order to engage a sales representative. Harry was willing to take some one-of-a-kind items to sell in his showroom. They looked interesting because they were different. He also used them at his booths in gift shows to attract buyers. In fact, when we first went to Harry we had only a few items to sell but he took us on.

Sales representatives often have contacts with large trading companies who may want you to buy for them abroad. For example, if you have exceptionally good taste, they may ask you to personally select one thousand pairs of mittens in New Zealand to assure getting a higher quality and better selection than might otherwise be chosen and they might pay you to do it. Sales representatives will also have a broader view of the market and would be able to tell you what sells and what does not. They might give you helpful hints about slight changes which will help a particular item to sell.

Often these people have a good sense of market trends and may be able to help you by letting you know the coming style in jewelry or whatever your market may be. Don't forget, they benefit from giving correct information. Sales representatives are constantly looking for new lines and better items to sell. They might develop one through you, so you will both make money. There is no reason to intentionally give you incorrect information. However, they may not genuinely know a market or may misread it completely—human errors that you yourself might make. One representative rejected our Spanish belts as being ugly and feeling they would not sell. Those belts became one of our most successful products. You may be able to sell one hundred of an item, but a sales representative, due to contacts, reputation and sales territory, may be able to sell ten thousand. You must be sure you can deliver. If your item is extremely good you will make enough to go back and fill the order personally. At this level importing is no longer an amateur activity. You're really in business.

A variant which we mentioned earlier is purchasing for museum collections. Museums have been known to be so interested in certain things from other countries to fill out one of their collections that they may even give you a brief course in how to find and verify those items. On one trip, we ran into a lovely California couple who were buying tapestries. The woman was from a small town and she had discussed her trip with the local museum prior to her departure. The museum had entrusted her with some of their funds to purchase a certain type of tapestry and spent time educating her on the methods of ascertaining the authenticity of the item. We met her again quite by accident upon our return. She said the museum was pleased with her purchases. She, too, was happy as she had purchased some similar textiles with her own funds, some of which she had retained and others she was able to sell for a good price because she knew they were authentic and was, as a result, able to speak intelligently and convincingly to buyers about their value.

≈ BUT HOW MUCH DO ≈ I SELL IT FOR?

So someone wants one of your rugs or necklaces. How much should you ask for it? In the final analysis, this is an individual decision, but there are some commonly understood guidelines to follow. Assuming that you are selling to a retail store, keep in mind that they will mark up their merchandise by more than doubling the wholesale (your price to them) cost. A general rule of thumb is that each person, each step of the way, tries to at least double their cost. For example, let us say that you purchase a skirt for $10, pay duty of $2, and freight charges of $1. Your total cost is, therefore, $13. (This, of course, for simplification, assumes no overhead costs.) Using our guidelines you should charge your customer at least $26 for the item and the store will more than double this as a final retail price of between $52 and $60. Is it worth that? If not, try to adjust your cost in either direction. For example, if you think it has a value of $100, you might ask a price of around $45 (for the store will charge $100, more than doubling the $45 cost to them). If it seems that the item should retail for $45, then you may have paid too much for it initially—however, you can still make a profit by selling it to the store for around $20 and you will have made approximately $7. You will have also learned a bit about your own buying.

Your friends may ask you to bring them something back, and, of course, offer to reimburse you for the cost, plus a little extra for your trouble. Think carefully about this, as you may lose a friend and end up with an inlaid box you don't want. If you do decide to take orders from friends, we suggest that you only bring back those things you would really like to have yourself or could sell easily elsewhere. Remember, friends do not always come through and it can be very difficult when they tell you, "Well, it is not exactly what I had in mind—you don't mind if I don't take it, do you?" This, after you spent *your* time and *your* money selecting the perfect Indonesian tribal mask *for them.*

If you sell to a friend, we suggest that you sell the item for at least what you would sell it for to a store. Your friend is receiving an incredible bargain by receiving a purchase for at least one-half of its retail cost. You have gone to the trouble of choosing the item, using your money as an investment and presenting it to someone. You should make a profit. You are in business. If you sell an item to a friend for $25 (what it cost you) and you could have sold it to a store for $50 (double) and they in turn have sold it for at least $100, your friend has saved more than $75 while you have lost the potential profit of $25 and reduced your inventory. Selling to friends can be a very tricky business—just remember that you are in business and must continue to make money in order to stay in the Game.

We feel that one of the most important things to keep in mind is that you need only start selling at a personal level, to your friends. Then if you feel like taking the plunge, know that these other options which we have discussed are open to you. If you do decide to go more public, be sure to check with a good accountant, your lawyer and your city and state officials to assure that you are proceeding legally.

And now you're back to the Start! You've bought the goods, sold them, and made some money! Isn't it time to take another trip?

Chapter Ten

THAT'S THE GAME!

That's the Importing Game! Like all games, it's simple to play once you've learned the basic rules. Once you've become comfortable with the Game, you can relax and enjoy it, and even start inventing variations—how about the Exporting Game?

When the dollar is low in relation to other currencies as when this was being written, how about taking American goods abroad? This is a little more difficult because it is harder for you to know about the rules applicable in the other countries and you have to be careful that you don't run into import quotas, high customs duties, exchange control regulations, and so forth. And of course, your market research is harder and actual marketing much more difficult. But think for a minute—what about those friends of yours abroad? Is there something you've taken abroad with you on which they have commented favorably? Can they think of some American products which they could sell easily in their country? Many inexpensive American consumer products would probably sell very well abroad, if someone bothered to export them. Your friend over there can help you determine whether a market exists and what problems might arise.

If you can find an export market you've doubled the profitability of your trip and equalized the trade balance. You've done your part for balanced trade, offset the cost of your trip, and had fun at the same time.

Another characteristic of a good game is that it is always fun. It's not limited to any one time or place but can be played throughout your life as circumstances and interests change. Perhaps prices in the places you are visiting are so high right now that purchases for resale aren't practicable. That doesn't mean the trip is a waste for purposes of the Importing Game. It just means that there won't be any profit from trading on this trip. But each time you look at and think about the salability of goods you see, you are honing your judgment. When you do see the salable bargain, you'll recognize it and until then you have refined your knowledge of the market and its opportunities.

So get started playing the Importing Game. We're sure you'll have fun. And it might just turn out to be profitable, too.

CUSTOMS HINTS FOR RETURNING U.S. RESIDENTS

KNOW BEFORE YOU GO

The U.S. Customs Service is proud of its role of protecting the interests of American citizens. And we ask for your support in carrying out this important task.

Customs' tradition of service is woven through our Nation's history. From 1789 to 1914 Customs revenues were virtually the only form of federal income. Customs revenues opened the West; purchased the Louisiana Territory, Florida and Alaska; paid for the first national road and the Transcontinental Railroad; built the U.S. Military and Naval Academies, the city of Washington, and the list goes on.

As the front-line U.S. revenue-producing law enforcement agency for 200 years, Customs enjoys a proud heritage of solid contribution to the American way of life. We ask you to join in our work in enforcing more than 400 laws for 40 agencies.

YOUR DECLARATION

You must declare all articles acquired abroad and in your possession at the time of your return. This includes:

- ❑ Articles that you purchased.
- ❑ Gifts presented to you while abroad, such as wedding or birthday presents.
- ❑ Articles purchased in duty-free shops.

- ❑ Repairs or alterations made to any articles taken abroad and returned, whether or not repairs or alterations were free of charge.
- ❑ Items you have been requested to bring home for another person.
- ❑ Any articles you intend to sell or use in your business.

In addition, you must declare any articles acquired in the U.S. Virgin Islands, American Samoa, or Guam and not accompanying you at the time of your return.

The price actually paid for each article must be stated on your declaration in U.S. currency or its equivalent in country of acquisition. If the article was not purchased, obtain an estimate of its fair retail value in the country in which it was acquired.

Note: The wearing or use of any article acquired abroad does not exempt it from duty. It must be declared at the price you paid for it. The Customs officer will make an appropriate reduction in its value for significant wear and use.

Oral Declaration

Customs declaration forms are distributed on vessels and planes and should be prepared in advance of arrival for presentation to the Immigration and Customs inspectors. Fill out the *identification* portion of the declaration form. You may declare orally to the Customs inspector the articles you acquired abroad if the articles are accompanying you and you have not exceeded the duty-free exemption allowed. A Customs officer may, however, ask you to prepare a written list if it is necessary.

Written Declaration

A written declaration will be necessary when:

- ❑ The total fair retail value of articles acquired abroad exceeds your personal exemption.

- ❑ More than one liter (33.8 fl. oz.) of alcoholic beverages, 200 cigarettes (one carton), or 100 cigars are included.
- ❑ Some of the items are not intended for your personal or household use, such as commercial samples, items for sale or use in your business, or articles you are bringing home for another person.
- ❑ Articles acquired in the U.S. Virgin Islands, American Samoa, or Guam are being sent to the U.S.
- ❑ A customs duty or internal revenue tax is collectible on any article in your possession.
- ❑ A Customs officer requests a written list.
- ❑ If you have used your exemption in the last 30 days.

Family Declaration

The head of a family may make a joint declaration for all members residing in the same household and returning *together to the United States.* Family members making a joint declaration may combine their personal exemptions, even if the articles acquired by one member of the family exceeds the personal exemption allowed.

Infants and children returning to the United States are entitled to the same exemptions as adults (except for alcoholic beverages). Children born abroad, who have never resided in the United States, are entitled to the customs exemptions granted nonresidents.

Warning: If you understate the value of an article you declare, or if you otherwise misrepresent an article in your declaration, you may have to pay a penalty in addition to payment of duty. Under certain circumstances, the article could be seized and forfeited if the penalty is not paid.

It is well known that some merchants abroad offer travelers invoices or bills of sale showing false or understated values. This practice not only delays your customs examination, but can prove very costly.

If you fail to declare an article acquired abroad, not only is the article subject to seizure and forfeiture, but you will be liable for a personal penalty in an amount equal to the value of the article in the United States. In addition, you may also be liable for criminal prosecution.

Don't rely on advice given by persons outside the Customs Service. It may be bad advice which could lead you to violate the customs laws and incur costly penalties.

If in doubt about whether an article should be declared, always declare it first and then direct your question to the Customs inspector. If in doubt about the value of an article, declare the article at the actual price paid (transaction value).

Customs inspectors handle tourist items day after day and become acquainted with the normal foreign values. Moreover, current commercial prices of foreign items are available at all times and on-the-spot comparisons of these values can be made.

Play it safe—avoid customs penalties.

YOUR EXEMPTIONS

In clearing U.S. Customs, a traveler is considered either a "returning resident of the United States" or a "nonresident."

Generally speaking, if you leave the United States for purposes of traveling, working or studying abroad and return to resume residency in the United States, you are considered a returning resident by Customs.

However, U.S. residents living abroad temporarily are entitled to be classified as nonresidents and thus receive more liberal Customs exemptions, on short visits to the United States, provided they export any foreign-acquired items at the completion of their visit.

Residents of American Samoa, Guam, or the U.S. Virgin Islands, who are American citizens, are also considered as returning U.S. residents.

Articles acquired abroad and brought into the United States are subject to applicable duty and internal revenue tax, but as a returning resident you are allowed certain exemptions from paying duty on items obtained while abroad.

$400 Exemption

Articles totaling $400 (based on the *fair retail value* of each item in the country where acquired) may be entered free of duty, subject to the limitations on liquors, cigarettes, and cigars, *if:*

- ❑ Articles were acquired as an incident of your trip for your personal or household use.
- ❑ You bring the articles with you at the time of your return to the United States and they are properly declared to Customs. *Articles purchased and left for alterations or other reasons cannot be applied to your $400 exemption when shipped to follow at a later date. The 10% flat rate of duty does not apply to mailed articles. Duty is assessed when received.*
- ❑ You are returning from a stay abroad of at least 48 hours. Example: A resident who leaves United States territory at 1:30 p.m. on June 1st would complete the required 48-hour period at 1:30 p.m. on June 3rd. This time limitation does not apply if you are returning from Mexico or the Virgin Islands of the U.S.
- ❑ You have not used this $400 exemption, or any part of it, within the preceding 30-day period. Also, your exemption is not cumulative. If you use a portion of your exemption on entering the United States, then you must wait for 30 days before you are entitled to another exemption other than a $25 exemption.
- ❑ Articles are not prohibited or restricted.

Cigars and Cigarettes: Not more than 100 cigars and 200 cigarettes (one carton) may be included in your exemption. Products of Cuban tobacco may be included if purchased in Cuba. This exemption is available to each person regardless of age.

Your cigarettes, however, may be subject to a tax imposed by state and local authorities.

Liquor: One liter (33.8 fl. oz.) of alcoholic beverages may be included in this exemption, *if:*

- ❑ You are 21 years of age or older.
- ❑ It is for your own use or for use as a gift.
- ❑ It is not in violation of the laws of the state in which you arrive.

Note: Most states restrict the quantity of alcoholic beverages you may import, and you must meet state alcoholic beverage laws in addition to federal ones. If the state in which you arrive permits less liquor than you have legally brought into the United States, that state's laws prevail.

Information about state restrictions and taxes should be obtained from the state government as laws vary from state to state.

Alcoholic beverages in excess of the one-liter limitation are subject to duty and internal revenue tax.

Shipping of alcoholic beverages by mail is prohibited by United States postal laws. Alcoholic beverages include wine and beer as well as distilled spirits.

$600 and $1200 Exemptions

If you return directly or indirectly from a U.S. insular possession—American Samoa, Guam, or the U.S. Virgin Islands—you may receive a customs exemption of $1200 (based upon the transaction value of the articles in the country where acquired). You may also bring in 1,000 cigarettes, but only 200 of them may have been acquired elsewhere.

Antigua and Baruda
Aruba
Bahamas
Barbados
Belize
Costa Rica
Dominica
Dominican Republic
El Salvador
Grenada
Guatemala
Guyan
Haiti
Honduras
Jamaica
Montserrat
Netherlands Antilles
Nicaragua
Panama
Saint Christopher/Kitts and Nevisa
Saint Lucia
Saint Vincent and the Grenadines
Trinidad and Tobago
Virgin Islands, British

If you are returning from any of the preceding 24 beneficiary countries, your customs exemption is $600, based upon fair market value.

In the case of the $1200 exemption, up to $600 worth of the merchandise may have been obtained in any of the beneficiary countries listed above, or up to $400 in any other country. For example, if you traveled to the U.S. Virgin Islands and Jamaica and then returned home, you would be entitled to bring in $1200 worth of merchandise duty free. Of this amount, $600 worth may have been acquired in Jamaica.

In the case of the $600 exemption, up to $400 worth of merchandise may have been acquired in other foreign countries. For instance, if you travel to England and the Bahamas, and then return home, your exemption is $600, $400 of which may have been acquired in England.

$25 Exemption

If you cannot claim the $400, $600, or $1200 exemptions, because of the 30-day or 48-hour minimum limitations, you may bring in free of duty and tax articles acquired abroad for your personal or household use if the total fair retail value does not exceed $25. This is an individual exemption and may not be grouped with other members of a family on one customs declaration.

You may include any of the following: 50 cigarettes, 10 cigars, 150 milliliters (4 fl. oz.) of alcoholic beverages, or 150 milliliters (4 fl. oz.) of alcoholic perfume. Cuban tobacco products brought directly from Cuba may be included.

Alcoholic beverages cannot be mailed into the United States. Customs enforces the liquor laws of the state in which you arrive. Because state laws vary greatly as to the quantity of alcoholic beverages which can be brought in, we suggest you consult the appropriate state authorities.

If any article brought with you is subject to duty or tax, or if the total value of all dutiable articles exceeds $25, no article may be exempted from duty or tax.

GIFTS

Bona fide gifts of not more than $50 in fair retail value where shipped can be received by friends and relations in the United States free of duty and tax, if the same person does not receive more than $50 in gift shipments in one day. The "day" in reference is the day in which the parcel(s) are received for customs processing. This amount is increased to $100 if shipped from the U.S. Virgin Islands, American Samoa, or Guam. These gifts are not declared by you upon your return to the States.

Gifts accompanying you are considered to be for your personal use and may be included within your exemption. This includes gifts given to you by others while abroad and those you intend to give to others after you return. Gifts intended for business, promotional or other commercial purposes may not be included.

Perfume containing alcohol valued at more than $5 retail, tobacco products, and alcoholic beverages are excluded from the gift provision.

Gifts intended for more than one person may be consolidated in the same package provided they are individually wrapped and labeled with the name of the recipient.

Be sure that the outer wrapping of the package is marked 1) unsolicited gift, 2) nature of the gift, and 3) its fair retail value. In addition, a consolidated gift parcel should be marked as such on the outside with the names of the recipients listed and the value of each gift. This will facilitate customs clearance of your package.

If any article imported in the gift parcel is subject to duty and tax, or if the total value of all articles exceeds the bona fide gift allowance, no article may be exempt from duty or tax.

If a parcel is subject to duty, the United States Postal Service will collect the duty plus a handling charge in the form of "Postage Due" stamps. Duty cannot be prepaid.

You, as a traveler, cannot send a "gift" parcel to yourself nor can persons traveling together send "gifts" to each other. Gifts ordered by mail from the United States do not qualify under this duty-free gift provision and are subject to duty.

OTHER ARTICLES: FREE OF DUTY OR DUTIABLE

Duty preferences are granted to certain developing countries under the Generalized System of Preferences (GSP). Some products from these countries have been exempted from duty which would otherwise be collected if imported from any other country. For details, obtain the leaflet *GSP & The Traveler* from your nearest Customs office. Many products of certain Caribbean countries are also exempt from duty under the Caribbean Basin Initiative (CBI). Most products of Israel may enter the United States either free of duty or at a reduced duty rate. Check with Customs.

The U.S.-Canada Free Trade Agreement was implemented on January 1, 1989. U.S. returning residents arriving directly or indirectly from Canada are eligible for free or reduced duty rates as applicable, on goods originating in Canada as defined in the Agreement.

Personal belongings of United States origin are entitled to entry free of duty. Personal belongings taken abroad, such as worn clothing, etc., may be sent home by mail before you return and receive free entry provided they have not been altered or repaired while abroad. These packages should be marked *"American Goods Returned."* When a claim of United States origin is made, marking on the article to so indicate facilitates customs processing.

Foreign-made personal articles taken abroad are dutiable each time they are brought into our country unless you have acceptable proof of prior possession. Documents which fully describe the article, such as a bill of sale, insurance policy, jeweler's appraisal, or receipt for purchase, may be considered reasonable proof of prior possession.

Items such as watches, cameras, tape recorders, or other articles which may be readily identified by serial number or permanently affixed markings, may be taken to the Customs office nearest you and registered before your departure. The Certificate of Registration provided will expedite free entry of these items when you return. Keep the certificate as it is valid for any future trips as long as the information on it remains legible.

Registration cannot be accomplished by telephone nor can blank registration forms be given or mailed to you to be filled out at a later time.

Automobiles, boats, planes, etc., or other vehicles taken abroad for noncommercial use may be returned duty free by proving to the Customs officer that you took them out of the United States. This proof may be the state registration card for an automobile, the Federal Aviation Administration certificate for an aircraft, a yacht license or motorboat identification certificate for a pleasure boat, or a customs Certificate of Registration obtained before departure.

Dutiable repairs or accessories acquired abroad for articles taken out of the United States must be declared on your return.

Warning: Catalytic-equipped vehicles (1976 or later model years) driven outside the United States, Canada, or Mexico will not, in most cases, meet EPA standards when brought back to the U.S. As unleaded fuel generally is not available in other countries, the catalytic converter will become inoperative and must be replaced. Contact Environmental Protection Agency, Washington, D.C. 20460, for details and exceptions.

Your local Customs office has the following leaflets which will be of interest—*Importing a Car and Pleasure Boats.* You may purchase *Customs Guide for Private Flyers* from your local Government Printing Office bookstore. Consult your local telephone book under "U.S. Government."

Household effects and tools of trade or occupation which you take out of the United States are duty free at the time you return if properly declared and entered.

All furniture, carpets, paintings, tableware, linens, and similar household furnishings acquired abroad may be imported free of duty, *if:*

- ❑ They are not imported for another person or for sale.
- ❑ They have been used abroad by you for not less than one year or were available for use in a household in which you were resident member for one year. This privilege does not include articles placed in storage outside the home. The year of use need not be continuous nor does it need to be the year immediately preceding the date of importation. Shipping time may not be included in the computation of the one year in use.

Items such as wearing apparel, jewelry, photograph equipment, tape recorders, stereo components, and vehicles are considered as personal articles and cannot be passed free of duty as household effects.

Articles imported in excess of your customs exemption will be subject to duty unless the items are entitled to free entry or prohibited.

The inspector will place the items having the highest rate of duty under your exemption, and duty will be assessed on the lower-rated items.

After deducting your exemptions and the value of any articles duty free, a flat rate of duty will be applied to the next $1,000 worth (fair retail value) of merchandise. Any dollar amount of an article or articles over $1,000 will be dutiable at the various rates of duty applicable to the articles.

Articles to which the flat rate of duty is applied must be for your personal use or for use as gifts and you cannot receive this flat rate provision more than once every 30 days, excluding the day of your last arrival.

The flat rate of duty is 5% for articles purchased in the U.S. Virgin Islands, American Samoa, or Guam, whether the articles accompany you or are shipped.

Example: You acquire goods valued at $2,500 from:

U.S. insular possessions:	
Personal exemption (free of duty)	up to $1,200
Flat duty rate at 5%	next $1,000
Various rates of duty remaining	$300
Total	$2,500

Caribbean Basin Economic Recovery Act countries:	
Personal exemption (free of duty)	up to $600
Flat duty rate at 10%	next $1,000
Various rates of duty	remaining $900
Total	$2,500

Other countries or locations:	
Personal exemption (free of duty)	up to $400
Flat duty rate at 10%	next $1,000
Various rates of duty	remaining $1,100
Total	$2,500

The flat rate of duty will apply to any articles which are dutiable and cannot be included in your personal exemption, even if you have not exceeded the dollar amount of your exemption. Example: You are returning from Europe with $200 worth of articles which includes 2 liters of liquor. One liter will be free of duty under your exemption, the other dutiable at 10%, plus any internal revenue tax.

Members of a family residing in one household traveling together on their return to the U.S. will group articles for application of the flat duty rate without regard as to which member of the family may be the owner of the articles.

Payment of duty, required at the time of your arrival on articles accompanying you, may be made by any of the following ways:

- ❑ U.S. currency (foreign is not acceptable).

- ❑ Personal check in the exact amount of duty, drawn on a national or state bank or trust company of the United States, made payable to the "U.S. Customs Service."
- ❑ Government check, money orders or traveler's checks are acceptable if they do not exceed the amount of the duty by more than $50. [Second endorsements are not acceptable. Identification must be presented; e.g. traveler's passport or driver's license.]
- ❑ In some locations you may pay duty with credit cards from Discover, Mastercard and VISA.

RATES OF DUTY

Various rates of duty for some of the more popular items imported by tourists are provided for use as an advisory guide only. If you have dutiable articles not subject to a flat rate of duty, the Customs officer examining your baggage will determine the rates of duty.

Rates of duty on imported goods are provided for in the Harmonized Tariff Schedule of the United States. There are two duty rates for each item, known as "column 1" and "column 2." Column 1 rates are those applicable to most favored nations. Column 2 rates are higher and apply to products from most Communist countries (exceptions: People's Republic of China, Hungary, Poland, Yugoslavia, and German Democratic Republic, now unified as one country with West Germany). Column 2 countries include:

Afghanistan	Albania
Bulgaria	Cuba*
Estonia	Kampuchea*
Laos	Latvia
Lithuania	Mongolia
North Korea*	Rumania
USSR	Vietnam

*Goods from, or products of, these countries are subject to foreign assets controls.

Eligible articles from Hungary, Poland, and Yugoslavia may be entered duty-free under the Generalized System of Preferences (GSP). These are GSP beneficiary countries.

Products of the above-listed column 2 countries are dutiable at the column 2 rates of duty, even if purchased in or sent from another country. Example: A crystal vase made in Rumania and purchased in Switzerland would be dutiable at the column 2 rate. If the article accompanies you, however, it may be entered under your duty-free personal exemption or the flat rate of duty allowance.

ALCOHOLIC BEVERAGES
(Subject to federal excise taxes, which greatly exceed Customs duties. These taxes vary from approximately 15 cents per liter for beer to more than $3.50 per proof liter for distilled spirits, liquors, and cordials.)

DISTILLED SPIRITS PER PROOF LITER	
Brandy	10.6¢ to 89.8¢
Gin	13.2¢
Liqueurs	13.2¢
Rum	37¢
Tequila	33¢ to 60¢
Vodka	13.2¢ to 67.6¢
Scotch	5.3¢
Other whiskeys	6.6¢
WINE PER LITER (33.814 fluid ounces)	
Sparkling	30.9¢
Still	8.3¢ to 26.4¢
BEER	1.6¢

ANTIQUES
Produced prior to 100 years before date of entry are admitted duty free. Have proof of antiquity obtained from seller.

AUTOMOBILES, Passenger	2.5%
BAGS, Hand, leather	5.3% to 10%
BEADS	
Imitation precious and semi-precious stone	8%
Ivory	4.7%

NOTE: Ivory beads made from elephant ivory are prohibited.

BINOCULARS (PRISM), OPERA and FIELD GLASSES	Free
BOOKS	Free
CAMERAS	
Motion picture	4.5%
Still, over $10 each	3%
Cases, leather	8%
Lenses, mounted	6.6%
NOTE: Cases imported with camera are classifiable with the camera.	
CANDY	
Sweetened chocolate bars	5%
Other	7%
CHESS SETS	4.64%
CHINA, other than tableware	
Bone	6.6%
Non-bone	2.5% to 9%
CHINA TABLEWARE	
Bone	8%
Non-bone, valued not over $56 per set	26%
Non-bone, valued over $56 per set	8%
CIGARETTE LIGHTERS	
Pocket	7.2% to 10%
Table	4.8%
CLOCKS, Valued over $5 each	45¢ + 6.4%
CRYSTAL	6% to 20%
DOLLS	
Stuffed	Check with Customs
Other	12%
DRAWINGS, done by hand	Free
FIGURINES, china (by professional sculptor)	3.1%
FILM	
Unexposed	3.7%
Exposed	Free
FUR	
Wearing apparel	5.8%

Item	Duty
Other	3.4%
NOTE: May be prohibited.	
FURNITURE	
Wood chairs	3.4% to 5.3%
Other than chairs	2.5%
Bentwood	6.6%
GOLF BALLS	2.4%
GLOVES	
Fur	5.8%
Horsehide or cowhide	14%
HANDKERCHIEFS, linen, hemmed	10.7%
IVORY, manufactured	4.2%
NOTE: May be prohibited as endangered species.	
JADE	
Cut, but not set, suitable for jewelry	2.1%
Other articles of jade	21%
JEWELRY, precious metal	
Silver chief value, valued not over $18 a doz.	27.5%
Other	6.5%
LEATHER	
Flatgoods, wallets	4.7% to 8%
Other manufactures of	Free to 5.6%
MUSIC BOXES	3.2%
PAINTINGS, done entirely by hand	Free
PEARLS	
Loose or temporarily strung without clasp:	
Natural	Free
Cultured	2.1%
Imitation	8%
Permanently strung or temporarily strung, with clasp attached or separate	6.5% to 11%
PERFUME	5%
NOTE: Subject to federal excise tax of $3.566322 per liter.	
POSTAGE STAMPS	Free
PRINTED MATTER	Free to 5.3%

Item	Rate
RADIOS, solid state radio receivers	6%
RECORDS, phonograph	3.7%
SHAVERS, electric	4.4%
SHELL ARTICLES NOTE: May be prohibited.	3.4%
SHOES, leather	2.5% to 20%
SKIS and SKI EQUIPMENT	3.5% to 5.5%
SOUND RECORDINGS	Free
STONES, cut but not set	
Diamonds	Free
Others	Free to 2.1%
SWEATERS, wool	7.5% to 17%
TAPE RECORDERS	3.9%
TOYS	7%
WATCHES	
Mechanical type (depending on jewels) plus	
Gold case	6.25%
Gold bracelet	14%
Digital type	3.9%
WEARING APPAREL	
Cotton, not knit	3% to 32%
Cotton, knit	7.9% to 21%
Linen, not knit	3% to 12%
Manmade fiber, knit	16.2% to 34.6%
Manmade fiber, not knit	7.6% to 52.9¢/Kg. + 21%
Silk, not knit	3% to 7.5%
Wool, knit	6% to 77.2¢/Kg. + 20%
Wool, not knit	9.8% to 30.4%
WOOD, carvings and articles of	5.1%

NOTE: Duty rates are subject to change without notice by statute. For further information call your nearest Customs District office.

PROHIBITED AND RESTRICTED ARTICLES

Because Customs inspectors are stationed at ports of entry and along our land and sea borders, they are often called upon to enforce laws and requirements of other Government agencies. For example, the Department of Agriculture is responsible for preventing the entry of injurious pest, plant, and animal diseases into the United States. The Customs officer cannot ignore the Agriculture requirements—the risk of costly damage to our crops, poultry and livestock industry is too great.

Certain articles considered injurious or detrimental to the general welfare of the United States are prohibited entry by law. Among these are *absinthe, liquor-filled candy (where prohibited by state law), lottery tickets, narcotics and dangerous drugs, obscene articles and publications, seditious and treasonable materials, hazardous articles (e.g., fireworks, dangerous toys, toxins or poisonous substances), and switchblade knives (however, a one-armed person may import a switchblade knife for personal use).*

Other items must meet special requirements before they can be released. You will be given a receipt for any articles retained by Customs.

Automobiles

Automobiles imported into the United States must conform to Environmental Protection Agency (EPA) emission standards and Department of Transportation (DOT) safety, bumper and theft prevention standards. Other than models required to meet theft prevention standards, vehicles may be entered conditionally to be brought into conformity. Automobiles that do not meet theft prevention standards will not be permitted entry into the United States, even under bond.

Automobiles that do not meet EPA emission standards can only be imported by holders of conformity certificates for EPA. These certificate holders are known as Independent Commercial Importers (ICI). Individuals contemplating purchasing a non-conforming vehicle should first make arrangements with an ICI for importing and modifying the vehicle to U.S. specifications.

Vehicles that do not meet DOT safety and bumper standards must be imported by a DOT-registered party under a DOT bond of one and one-half times the value of the vehicle. Bonds may be difficult to obtain and can be expensive. Security deposits of 50% or more of the bond amount may be required.

Vehicles that do not conform to either EPA or DOT standards must be imported by a company that is an ICI and DOT-registered party with a separate DOT bond for one and one-half times the value of the vehicle.

Prospective purchasers should be aware that almost all automobiles purchased overseas are manufactured to European specifications and will require modification. Vehicles imported conditionally to be modified to U.S. specifications, and not modified, or not modified acceptably, must either be exported or destroyed under Customs supervision.

Further information on importing vehicles may be obtained from the Environmental Protection Agency, Attn: EN-340F, Washington, D.C. 20460, telephone (202) 382-2504, and the Department of Transportation, Office of Vehicle Safety Compliance (NEF 32), Washington, D.C. 20590. Copies of the Customs pamphlet *Importing a Car* and the EPA brochure *Buying a Car Overseas? Beware!* may be obtained by contacting the publishing agency.

Biological Materials

Biological materials of public health or veterinary importance (disease organisms and vectors for research and educational purposes) require import permits. Write to the Foreign Quarantine Program, U.S. Public Health Service, Center for Disease Control, Atlanta, GA 30333.

Books, Records, Computer Programs and Cassettes

"Piratical" copies of copyrighted articles—unlawfully made articles produced without the authorization of the copyright owner—are prohibited from importation into the United States. Piratical copies will be seized and destroyed, unless the importer can demonstrate that he had no reasonable grounds for believing his actions violated the law. Then, they may only be returned to the country of export.

Ceramic Tableware

Some ceramic tableware sold abroad contains dangerous levels of lead in the glaze that can leach into certain foods and beverages served in them. The Food and Drug Administration recommends that ceramic tableware, especially when purchased in Mexico, the People's Republic of China, Hong Kong or India, be tested for lead release on your return or be used for decorative purposes only.

Cultural Property

An export certificate issued by certain Latin American countries may be required in order to import pre-Columbian monumental and architectural sculpture and murals, whether they are shipped directly or indirectly from the country of origin to the United States. Currently, there are import restrictions on certain items from Peru, Bolivia, and El Salvador. Customs also enforces the Convention on Cultural Property Implementation Act. The regulations prohibit illicit traffic in cultural property while allowing the exchange of national treasures for legitimate scientific, educational, and cultural purposes. For further information, contact the United States Information Agency, Washington, D.C. (202) 485-6612.

Drug Paraphernalia

The importation, exportation, manufacture, sale and transportation of drug paraphernalia are prohibited. Persons convicted of these offenses are subject to fines and imprisonment. As importations contrary to law, drug paraphernalia may be seized by U.S. Customs.

Firearms and Ammunition

Firearms and ammunition are subject to restrictions and import permits approved by the Bureau of Alcohol, Tobacco and Firearms (ATF). Applications to import may be made only by or through a licensed importer, dealer, or manufacturer. Weapons, ammunition, or other devices prohibited by the National Firearms Act will not be admitted into the United States unless specifically authorized by ATF.

No import permit is required when it is proven that the firearms or ammunition were previously taken out of the United States by the person who is returning with such firearms or ammunition. To facilitate *reentry,* persons may have them registered before departing from the United States at any Customs office or ATF field office. However, not more than three nonautomatic firearms and 1,000 cartridges therefore, will be registered for any one person. Quantities beyond these are subject to the export licensing requirements of the Office of Munitions Control, Department of State, Washington, D.C. 20520.

For further information, contact the Bureau of Alcohol, Tobacco and Firearms, Department of the Treasury, Washington, D.C. 20226.

Residents of the United States carrying firearms or ammunition with them to other countries should consult in advance the customs officials or the respective embassies of those countries as to their regulations.

Food Products

Bakery items and all cured cheeses are admissible. The USDA Animal and Plant Health Inspection Service leaflet, *Travelers' Tips,* provides detailed information on bringing food, plant, and animal products into the U.S. Imported foods are also subject to requirements of the Food and Drug Administration.

Fruits and Vegetables

Most fruits and vegetables are either prohibited from entering the country or require an import permit. Every fruit or vegetable must be declared to the Customs officer and must be presented for inspection, no matter how free of pests it appears to be. Most canned or processed items are admissible.

Applications for import permits or requests for information should be addressed to Quarantines, USDA-APHIS-PPQ, Federal Building, 6505 Belcrest Road, Hyattsville, MD 20782.

Gold

Gold coins, medals, and bullion, formerly prohibited, may be brought into the U.S.; however, copies of gold coins are prohibited if not properly marked. (Mexico restricts export of gold and gold coins. Contact Mexican Customs; the United States prohibits importation of Krugerrands and Soviet gold coins; check with U.S. Customs.)

Meats, Livestock, Poultry

Meats, livestock, poultry, and their by-products (such as sausage, paté) are either prohibited or restricted from entering the United States, depending on the animal disease condition in country of origin. Fresh meat is generally prohibited from most countries. Canned meat is permitted if the inspector can determine that it is commercially canned, cooked in the container, hermetically sealed, and can be kept without refrigeration. Other canned, cured, or dried meat is severely restricted from most countries.

All prohibited importations will be seized and destroyed unless the importer returns them immediately to their country of origin.

You should contact USDA-APHIS-PPQ, Federal Building, 6505 Belcrest Road, Hyattsville, MD 20782, for detailed requirements or call (301) 436-7472.

Medicine/Narcotics

Narcotics and dangerous drugs, including anabolic steroids, are prohibited entry and there are severe penalties if imported. A traveler requiring medicines containing habit-forming drugs or narcotics (e.g., cough medicines, diuretics, heart drugs, tranquilizers, sleeping pills, depressants, stimulants, etc.) should:

- ❑ Have all drugs, medicinals, and similar products properly identified;
- ❑ Carry only such quantity as might normally be carried by an individual having some sort of health problem;
- ❑ Have either a prescription of written statement from your personal physician that the medicinals are being used under a doctor's direction and are necessary for your physical well-being while traveling.

Warning: The Food and Drug Administration prohibits the importation, by mail or in person, of fraudulent prescription and non-prescription drugs and medical devices. These may include unorthodox "cures" for medical conditions including cancer, AIDS, and multiple sclerosis. While these drugs and devices may be completely legal elsewhere, they may not have been approved for use in the United States, even under a prescription issued by a foreign physician. The may not legally enter the United States and may be confiscated upon arrival by mail.

For additional information, contact your nearest FDA office or write Food and Drug Administration, Import Operations Unit, Room 12-8 (HFC-131), 5600 Fishers Lane, Rockville, MD 20857.

Merchandise

The importation of merchandise or goods that contain components from the following countries is generally prohibited under regulations administered by the Office of Foreign Assets Control: Cambodia, Cuba, Iran, Iraq, Libya, North Korea, and Vietnam. Importation of all merchandise produced, grown, manufactured, marketed, or exported by any public or quasi-governmental South African agency is prohibited. In addition, agricultural commodities, derivatives, and articles suitable for human consumption, textiles, gold, and Krugerrands from South Africa are also prohibited imports.

These proscriptions do not apply to informational materials such as pamphlets, books, tapes, films, or recordings.

Specific licenses are required to bring prohibited merchandise into the United States; but they are rarely granted. Foreign visitors to the United States, however, may be permitted to bring in small articles for personal use as accompanied baggage, depending upon the goods' country of origin.

Travelers should be aware of certain travel restrictions that may apply to these countries. Because of the strict enforcement of these prohibitions, those anticipating foreign travel to any of the countries listed above would do well to write in advance to the Office of Foreign Assets Control, Department of the Treasury, Washington, D.C. 20220, or to call (202) 566-2701.

Money and Other Monetary Instruments

There is no limitation in terms of total amount of monetary instruments which may be brought into or taken out of the United States nor is it illegal to do so. However, if you transport or cause to be transported (including by mail or other means) more than $10,000 in monetary instruments on any occasion into or out of the United States, or if you receive more than that amount, you must file a report (Customs Form 4790) with the U.S. Customs (Currency & Foreign Transactions Reporting Act, 31 U.S.C. 1101, et seq.). Failure to comply can result in civil and criminal penalties. Monetary instruments include U.S. or foreign coin in current circulation, currency, traveler's checks in any form, money orders, and negotiable instruments or investment securities in bearer form.

Pets

There are controls, restrictions, and prohibitions on entry of animals, birds, turtles, wildlife, and endangered species. Cats and dogs must be free of evidence of diseases communicable to man. Vaccination against rabies is not required for cats and dogs arriving from rabies-free countries. Personally owned pet birds may be entered (limit of two if of the psittacine family), but APHIS and Public Health Service requirements must be met, including quarantine at any APHIS facility at specified locations, at the owner's expense. Advance reservations are required. Non-human primates, such as monkeys, apes, and similar animals, may not be imported. If you plan to take your pet abroad, or import one on your return, obtain a copy of our leaflet, *Pets, Wildlife, U.S. Customs.*

You should check with state, county, and municipal authorities about any restrictions and prohibitions they may have before importing a pet.

Plants

Plants, cuttings, seeds, unprocessed plant products and certain endangered species either require an import permit or are prohibited from entering the United States. Endangered or threatened species of plants and plant products, if importation is not prohibited, will require an export permit from the country of origin. Every single plant or plant product must be declared to the Customs officer and must be presented for inspection, no matter how free of pests it appears to be. Applications for import permits or requests for information should be addressed to: Quarantines, USDA-APHIS-PPQ, Federal Building, 6505 Belcrest Road, Hyattsville, MD 20782.

Textiles

Textile and apparel items which accompany you and which you have acquired abroad for personal use or as gifts are generally not subject to quantitative restrictions. However, unaccompanied textile and apparel items may be subject to certain quantitative restrictions (quotas) which require a document called a "visa" or "export license" or exempt certificate as appropriate from the country of production. Check with Customs before you depart on your trip.

Trademarked Articles

Foreign-made trademarked articles may be limited as to the quantity which may be brought into the United States if the registered trademark has been recorded by an American trademark owner with U.S. Customs.

The types of articles usually of interest to tourists are 1) lenses, cameras, binoculars, optical goods; 2) tape recorders, musical instruments; 3) jewelry, precious metalware; 4) perfumery; 5) watches, clocks.

Persons arriving in the United States with a trademarked article are allowed an exemption, usually one article of a type bearing a protected trademark. An exempted trademark article must accompany you, and you can claim this exemption for the same type of article only once each 30 days. The article must be for your personal use and not for sale. If an exempted article is sold within one year following importation, the article or its value is subject to forfeiture.

If the trademark owner allows a quantity in excess of the aforementioned exemption for its particular trademarked article, the total of those trademarked articles authorized may be entered. Articles bearing counterfeit trademarks, if the amount of such articles exceeds the traveler's personal exemption, are subject to seizure and forfeiture.

For additional information on trademarked merchandise, consult our leaflet *Trademark Information for Travelers.*

Wildlife and Fish

Wildlife and fish are subject to certain import and export restrictions, prohibitions, permits or certificates, and quarantine requirements. This includes:

- ❑ Wild birds, mammals including marine mammals, reptiles, crustaceans, fish, and mollusks.
- ❑ Any part or product, such as skins, feathers, eggs.
- ❑ Products and articles manufactured from wildlife and fish.

Endangered species of wildlife and products made from them are prohibited from being imported or exported. All ivory and ivory products—except antiques—made from elephant ivory are prohibited. Ivory antiques may be imported provided they can be documented as being 100 years old. (Certain other requirements for antiques may apply.) If you contemplate purchasing articles made from wildlife, such as tortoise shell jewelry, leather goods, or other articles made from whalebone, ivory, skins, or fur, please contact—before you go—the U.S. Fish and Wildlife Service, Department of the Interior, Washington, D.C. 20240 which also prescribes the limits on migratory game birds, prior to each hunting season. Ask for their pamphlet *Fish and Wildlife.*

If you plan to import fish or wildlife, or any product, article or part, check with Customs or Fish and Wildlife Service first, as only certain ports are designated to handle these entries. Additional information is contained in our leaflet, *Pets, Wildlife, U.S. Customs.*

Federal regulations do not authorize the importation of any wildlife or fish into any state of the United States if the state's laws or regulations are more restrictive than any applicable Federal treatment. Wild mammals or birds taken, killed, sold, possessed, or exported to the United States in violation of any foreign laws are not allowed entry into the United States.

CUSTOMS POINTERS

Traveling Back and Forth Across Border

After you have crossed the United States boundary at one point and you swing back into the United States to travel to another point in the foreign country, you run the risk of losing your customs exemption unless you meet certain requirements. If you make a "swing back," don't risk your exemptions—ask the nearest Customs officer about these requirements.

"Duty-Free" Shops

Articles bought in "duty-free" shops in foreign countries are subject to U.S. customs duty and restrictions but may be included in your personal exemption.

Articles purchased in U.S. "duty-free" shops are subject to U.S. customs duty if reentered into the U.S. Example: Liquor bought in a "duty-free" shop before entering Canada and brought back into the United States will be subject to duty and internal revenue tax.

Note: Many travelers are confused by the term "duty free" as it relates to shops. Articles sold in duty-free shops are free of duty and taxes only *for the country in which that shop is located.* Articles sold in duty-free shops are intended for export and are not to be returned to the country of purchase. Thus, for example, if you were to buy a Hermes scarf in Orly Airport's duty-free shop, the price you pay will not include the tax you would have to pay if you bought that same scarf at Hermes in Faubourg St. Honore. So if your purchases exceed your personal exemption, that scarf may not be duty free for you.

Keep Your Sales Slips

You will find your sales slips, invoices, or other evidence of purchase not only helpful when making out your declaration, but necessary if you have unaccompanied articles being sent from the U.S. Virgin Islands, American Samoa, Guam, or any of the Caribbean Basin countries.

Packing Your Baggage

Pack your baggage in a manner that will make inspection easy. Do your best to pack separately the articles you have acquired abroad. When the Customs officer asks you to open your luggage or the trunk of your car, please do so without hesitation.

Photographic Film

All imported photographic films, which accompany a traveler, if not for commercial purpose, may be released without examination by Customs unless there is reason to believe they contain objectionable matter.

Films prohibited from entry are those that contain obscene matter, advocate treason or insurrection against the United States, advocate forcible resistance to any law of the United States, or those that threaten the life of or infliction of bodily harm upon any person in the United States.

Developed or undeveloped U.S. film exposed abroad (except motion-picture film to be used for commercial purposes) may enter free of duty and need not be included in your customs exemption.

Foreign film purchased abroad and prints made abroad are dutiable but may be included in your customs exemption.

Shipping Hints

Merchandise acquired abroad may be sent home by you or by the store where purchased. *As these items do not accompany you on your return, they cannot be included in your customs exemption and are subject to duty when received in the United States. Duty cannot be prepaid.* There are, however, special procedures to follow for merchandise acquired in and sent from the U.S. Virgin Islands, American Samoa, Guam or Caribbean Basin countries.

All incoming shipments must be cleared through U.S. Customs. Customs employees cannot, by law, perform entry tasks for the importing public, but they will advise and give information to importers about customs requirements.

Customs collects customs duty (if any) as provided for in the tariff schedule, certain Internal Revenue taxes and several user fees amounting to less than one percent of the value. Any other charges paid on import shipments are for handling by freight forwarders, commercial brokers, or for other delivery services. Some carriers may add other clearance charges that have nothing to do with Customs duties.

Note: Customs brokers are not U.S. Customs employees. Fees charged by the brokers are based on the amount of work done, not on the value of the personal effects or of the tourist purchase you shipped. The fee may seem excessive to you in relation to the value of the shipment. The National Customs Brokers & Forwarders Association is well aware of the difficulties and excessive expense incurred by tourists shipping items home. Their advice is "Ship the easy way—take it with you in your baggage or send it by parcel post prepaid."

Mail Shipments (including parcel post) have proven to be more convenient and less costly for travelers. Parcels must meet the mail requirements of the exporting country as to weight, size, or measurement.

The U.S. Postal Service sends all incoming foreign mail shipments to Customs for examination. Packages free of customs duty are returned to the Postal Service for delivery to you by your home post office without additional postage, handling costs, or other fees.

For packages containing dutiable articles, the Customs officer will attach a mail entry showing the amount of duty to be paid and return the parcel to the Postal Service. The duty and a postal handling fee will be collected when the package is delivered. In addition, there is a $5 Customs processing fee on dutiable packages.

Formal entry may be required for some shipments (some textiles, wearing apparel and small leather goods) regardless of value. Customs employees cannot prepare this type of entry for you. Only you or a licensed customs broker may prepare a formal entry.

If you pay the duty on a package but feel that the duty was not correct, you may file a protest. This protest can be acted on only by the Customs office which issued the mail entry receipt—Customs Form 3419—attached to your package. Send a copy of this form with your protest letter to the Customs office at the location and address shown on the left side of the form. That office will review the duty assessment based on the information furnished in your letter and, if appropriate, authorize a refund.

Another procedure would be to not accept the parcel. You would then have to provide, within 30 days, a written statement of your objections to the Postmaster where the parcel is being held. Your letter will be forwarded to the issuing Customs office. The shipment will be detained at the post office until a reply is received.

Express shipments may be sent to the United States from Canada and Mexico and by airfreight from other countries. The express company usually provides or arranges for customs clearance of the merchandise for you. A fee is charged for this service.

Freight shipments, whether or not they are free of duty at the time of importation, must clear customs at the first port of arrival into the united states, or, if you choose, the merchandise may be forwarded in customs custody (in bond) from the port of arrival to another customs port of entry for customs clearance.

All arrangements for customs clearance and forwarding in bond must be made by you or someone you designate to act for you. Frequently, a freight forwarder in a foreign country will handle all the necessary arrangements, including the clearance through Customs in the United States by a customs broker. A fee is charged for this service. This fee is not a Customs charge. If a foreign seller consigns a shipment to a broker or agent in the United States, the freight charge is usually paid only to the first port of arrival in the United States. This means there will be additional inland transportation or freight forwarding charges, brokers' fees, insurance, and other items.

An individual may also effect the customs clearance of a single, noncommercial shipment not requiring formal entry for you, if it is not possible for you to personally secure the release of the goods. You must authorize and empower the individual in writing to execute the customs declaration and the entry for you as your unpaid agent. The written authority provided to the individual should be addressed to the "Officer in Charge of Customs" at the port of entry.

Unaccompanied tourist purchases acquired in and sent directly from the U.S. Virgin Islands, American Samoa, Guam, or a Caribbean Basin country, may be entered, if properly declared and processed, as follows:

- Up to $1200 free of duty under your personal exemption if from an insular possession; $600 if from a Caribbean Basin country. Remember that if up to $400 of this amount was acquired elsewhere than these countries, those articles must accompany you at the time of your return in order to claim duty-free entry under your personal exemption.
- An additional $1,000 worth of articles, dutiable at a flat 5 percent rate if from an insular possession, or a flat 10 percent rate if the merchandise is from a Caribbean Basin country.
- Any amount over the above, dutiable at various rates of duty.

The procedure outlined below must be followed:

Step 1. You will: a) list all articles acquired abroad on your baggage declaration (Customs Form 6059B) except those sent under the $50 *or* the $100 bona fide gift provision to friends and relatives in the U.S.; b) indicate which articles are unaccompanied; c) fill out a Declaration of Unaccompanied Articles (Customs Form 255) for each package or container to be sent. This form may be obtained when you clear Customs if it was not available where you made your purchase.

Step 2. Customs at the time of your return will: a) collect duty and tax if owed on goods accompanying you; b) verify your unaccompanied articles against sales slips, invoices, etc.; c) validate Form 255 as to whether goods are free of duty under your personal exemption or subject to a flat rate of duty. Two copies of the three-part form will be returned to you.

Step 3. You will return the yellow copy of the form to the shopkeeper (or vendor) holding your purchase and keep the other copy for your records. You are responsible for advising the shopkeeper at the time you make your purchase that your package is not to be sent until this form is received.

Step 4. The shopkeeper will place the form in an envelope and attach the envelope securely to the outside of the package or container, which must be clearly marked "Unaccompanied Tourist Purchase." *Please note that a form must be placed on each box or container.* This is the most important step to be followed in order for you to receive the benefits allowed under this procedure.

Step 5. The Postal Service will deliver the package, if sent by mail, to you after Customs clearance. Any duty owed will be collected by the Postal Service plus a postal handling fee; or you will be notified by the carrier as to the arrival of your shipment at which time you will go to the Customs office processing your shipment and make entry. Any duty or tax owed will be paid at that time. You may employ a customs broker to do this for you. A fee will be charged by the broker.

Storage charges. Freight and express packages delivered before you return (without prior arrangements for acceptance) will be placed in storage by Customs after five days, at the expense and risk of the owner. If not claimed within one year, the items will be sold.

Mail parcels not claimed within 30 days will be returned to the sender unless a duty assessment is being protested.

Notice to California Residents

California residents should know that merchandise purchased abroad and brought back to California may be subject to a "use tax." On October 1, 1990, California began to assess a use tax on these purchases, using information from Customs declarations completed by returning travelers at ports of entry. The use-tax rate is the same as the sales-tax rate in the traveler's California county of residence.

For more information about the use-tax program, contact the California Board of Equalization's Occasional Sales Use Tax Unit, (916) 445-9524.

FOR FURTHER INFORMATION

Every effort has been made to indicate essential requirements; however, all regulations of Customs and other agencies cannot be covered in full. Customs offices will be glad to advise you of any changes in regulations which may have occurred since publication of this leaflet.

District Directors of Customs are located in the following cities:

Anchorage, Alaska 99501	907/271-4043
Baltimore, Md. 21202	301/962-2666
Boston, Mass. 02222-1059	617/565-6147
Buffalo, NY 14202	716/846-4373
Charleston, SC 29402	803/724-4312
Charlotte Amalie; St. Thomas-V.I. 00801	809/774-2530
Chicago, Ill. 60607	312/353-6100
Cleveland, Ohio 44114	216/522-4284
Dallas/Ft. Worth, Tex. 75261	214/574-2170

Detroit, Mich. 48226-2568 313/226-3177
Duluth, Minnesota 55802-1390 218/720-5201
El Paso, Texas 79985 915/534-6798
Great Falls, Montana 59405 406/453-7631
Honolulu, Hawaii 96806 808/541-1725
Houston, Texas 77029 713/671-1000
Laredo, Texas 78041-3130 512/726-2267
Los Angeles/Long Beach, CA 90731 213/514-6001
Miami, Florida 33131 305/536-5791
Milwaukee, Wisconsin 53237-0260 414/297-3925
Minneapolis, Minnesota 55401 612/348-1690
Mobile, Alabama 36602 205/690-2106
New Orleans, Louisiana 70130 504/589-6353
New York Seaport Area,
New York, New York 10048 212/466-5817
Kennedy Airport Area,
Jamaica, New York 11430 718/917 1542
Newark Area, Newark, New Jersey 07114 201/645-3760
Nogales, Arizona 85621 602/287-3637
Norfolk, Virginia 23510 804/441-6546
Ogdensburg, New York 13669 315/393-0660
Pembina, North Dakota 58271 701/825-6201
Philadelphia, Pennsylvania 19106 215/597-4605
Port Arthur, Texas 77642 409/724-0087
Portland, Maine 04112 207/780-3326
Portland, Oregon 97209 503/221-2865
Providence, Rhode Island 02905 401/528-5080
St. Albans, Vermont 05478 802/524-6527
St. Louis, Missouri 63105 314/425-3134
San Diego, California 92188 619/557-5360
San Francisco, California 94126 415/465-4340
San Juan, Puerto Rico 00901 809/729-6950
Savannah, Georgia 31401 912/944-4256
Seattle, Washington 98174 206/442-0554
Tampa, Florida 33605 813/228-2381
Washington, D.C. 20041, Washington Dulles
Intl. Airport, Chantilly, Va. 22021 202/661-3600
Wilmington, North Carolina 28401 919/343-4601

Preclearance Offices

Montreal	514/636-3859
Toronto	416/676-3399
Winnipeg	204/783-2206
Calgary	403/221-1733
Edmonton	403/890-4514
Vancouver	604/278-1825
Bermuda	809/293-0353
Nassau	809/327-7126
Freeport	809/352-7256

Customs Assistance Abroad. Should you need Customs assistance while abroad, you can visit or telephone our representatives located at the American Embassy or consulate in:

Bangkok	662/252-5040
Bonn	49/228/339-2207
Dublin	353/1/688777
The Hague	31/70/924-651
Hermosillo	52/621-75258
Hong Kong	852/2/239-011
London	44/1/499-9000
Merida	52/99/258235
Mexico City	(525)211-0042
Milan	39/2/655-4973
Monterrey	52/83/45/2120
Ottawa	(613)238-5335
Panama City	507/271-777
Paris	33/1/4296-1202
Rome	39/6/4674-2475
Seoul	822/732-2601
Singapore	65/338-0251
Tokyo	81/3/224-5435
Vienna	43/222/31-55-11

Ask for the U.S. customs service.

Frequently, we are asked questions which are not Custom matters. If you want to know about . . .

Passports. Contact the Passport Agency nearest you at the following zip codes:

Boston	02203-0123
Chicago	60604-1564
Honolulu	96850
Houston	77002-4874
Los Angeles	90024-3614
Miami	33130-1680
New Orleans	70113-1931
New York	10111-0031
Philadelphia	19106-1684
San Francisco	94105-2773
Seattle	98174-1091
Stamford, CT	06901-2767
Washington, D.C.	20524-0002

Some of the Clerks of Court and Postal Clerks also accept passport applications.

Baggage Allowance. Ask the airline or steamship line you are travelling on about this.

Currency of Other Nations. Your local bank can help.

Foreign Countries. For information about the country you will visit or about what articles may be taken into that country, contact the appropriate Embassy, consular office, or tourist information center.

Department of the Treasury
U.S. Customs Service
Washington, D.C. 20229
Customs Publication No. 512
Revised March 1991

GENERALIZED SYSTEM OF PREFERENCES

GSP AND THE TRAVELER

QUESTIONS AND ANSWERS

What is GSP?
GSP (Generalized System of Preferences) is a system used by many developed countries to help *developing* nations improve their financial or economic condition through export trade. In effect, it provides for the duty-free importation of a wide range of products from certain countries, which would otherwise be subject to customs duty.

When did GSP go into effect for the United States?
GSP went into effect on January 1, 1976. It was renewed on October 9, 1984, and will remain in effect until July 4, 1993.

How is GSP administered?
GSP is administered by the United States Trade Representative in consultation with the Secretary of State. The duty suspensions are proclaimed by the President under the Trade Act of 1974 as amended. The U.S. Customs Service is responsible for determining eligibility for duty-free entry under GSP.

What products are eligible?

Approximately 4,100 items have been designated as eligible for duty-free treatment from beneficiary developing countries (BDCs). The eligible articles are identified in the Harmonized Tariff Schedule of the United States Annotated and the designated countries are also listed therein.

For the traveler's convenience, an advisory list of the most popular tourist items which, in general, have been accorded GSP status is included in this leaflet.

Are certain items excluded?

Under the Trade Act, many items such as most footwear, most textile articles (including clothing), watches, some electronic products, and certain glass and steel products are specifically excluded from GSP benefits.

What countries have been designated as BDCs?

Approximately 130 countries and territories have been designated.

Are the articles and countries subject to change?

Yes. Articles may be excluded by Executive Order if it is determined that their importation is harmful to domestic industry. Beneficiary countries may also be excluded from the GSP program at any time, due to other trade considerations.

In addition, some articles from specified countries may be excluded from GSP treatment, if during the preceding year:

- the level of imports of those articles exceeded a specific dollar limit indexed to the nominal growth of the U.S. gross national product, since 1984.
- that country supplied 50 percent or more of the total U.S. imports of that product.

Are there any specific requirements or qualifications I must be aware of to be sure an article qualifies for duty-free treatment?
In order to take advantage of GSP, you must have acquired the eligible article in the same beneficiary country where it was grown, manufactured, or produced. Articles may accompany you or may be shipped from the developing country *directly* to the United States.

What forms are required?
On goods valued at more than $1000, the District Director of Customs may require a Certificate of Origin (Form A), whether you ship the goods or bring them with you. If shipped, the goods should be accompanied by a commercial invoice in addition to Form A. This form would normally be obtained from the seller of the eligible article.

What about merchandise acquired in duty-free shops?
Most items purchased in duty-free shops will not be eligible for GSP treatment unless the merchandise was produced in the country in which the duty-free shop is located.

What about Internal Revenue tax?
Such items as gin, liqueur, perfume, if designated as eligible articles, may be subject to Internal Revenue Service tax despite their GSP status.

What happens if I thought an article was eligible for duty-free entry and it is not?
When merchandise claimed to be free of duty under GSP is found to be dutiable, you may include it in your customs exemption. Articles imported in excess of your exemption will be subject to duty. If you feel your article should have been passed free of duty, you may write to the District Director of Customs where you entered, giving him the information concerning your entry. He will make a determination as to whether you are due a refund.

Am I still entitled to my basic customs exemption?
As a returning U.S. resident, you may still bring in free of duty $400 worth of articles (fair retail value) acquired abroad in addition to those items covered by GSP. This exemption is $1,200 if you are returning from the U.S. Virgin Islands, American Samoa, or Guam, and $600 if you are returning from certain Caribbean Basin Initiative beneficiary countries. Remember that all articles acquired abroad, whether free of duty or not, including those entitled to GSP, must be declared to U.S. Customs on your return.

Visitors or nonresidents are entitled to bring in articles which are duty free under GSP in addition to their basic customs exemption.

Whom Should I contact if I have any questions about GSP?
Contact your nearest U.S. Customs office—there are almost 300 ports of entry throughout the United States. If you are overseas, the U.S. Embassy or consulate can be of assistance.

POPULAR TOURIST ITEMS

This listing is solely an advisory guide to items designated as eligible for duty-free treatment under GSP which may be of interest to travelers for their personal use. Note that certain items, if from a particular beneficiary country, may be excluded. Do not hesitate to check with your nearest Customs office or the American Embassy or consulate in the country you are visiting to verify the GSP status of any article you are considering bringing into the United States.

BASKETS or bags of bamboo, willow or rattan.

CAMERAS, motion-picture and still; lenses; and other photographic equipment.

CANDY

CHINAWARE, bone: household ware; and other articles such as vases, statues, figurines; non-bone: articles other than household ware (except for non-bone chinaware or subporcelain).

CIGARETTE LIGHTERS, pocket and table.

CORK, manufactures of.

EARTHENWARE or stoneware except household ware available in sets.

FLOWERS, artificial of plastic or feathers.

FURNITURE of wood, rattan, or plastic.

GAMES, played on boards: chess, backgammon, darts, Mah-Jongg.

GOLF BALLS and EQUIPMENT

IVORY, beads; other manufactures of ivory.

JADE, cut but not set for use in jewelry and other articles of jade.

JEWELRY of precious metal, of precious stones, or of precious metal set with semi-precious stones, cameos, intaglios, amber, or coral: Silver, chief value, valued not over $18 per dozen. Necklaces and neck chains, almost wholly of gold: except rope from Israel and mixed link.

JEWELRY BOXES, unlined.

MUSIC BOXES and MUSICAL INSTRUMENTS

PAPER, manufactures of.

PEARLS, cultured or imitation, loose or temporarily strung and without clasp.

PERFUME

PRINTED MATTER

RADIO RECEIVERS, solid state (not for motor vehicles).

RECORDS, phonograph and tapes.

SHAVERS, electric.

SHELL, manufactures of.

SILVER, tableware and flatware.

SKIS and SKI EQUIPMENT, ski boots not included.

STONES, cut but not set, suitable for use in jewelry. Precious and semi-precious stones including marcasites; coral and cameos.

TAPE RECORDERS

TOILET PREPARATIONS

TOYS

WIGS

WOOD, carvings.

BENEFICIARY COUNTRIES

The countries listed below are designated as beneficiary developing countries in the U.S. Generalized System of Preferences.

Angola
§Antigua and Barbuda***
Argentina
§Aruba
§Bahamas***
Bahrain
Bangladesh
§Barbados***
§Belize***
Benin
Bhutan
Bolivia*
Botswana
Brazil
Burkina Faso
Burundi
Cameroon
Cape Verde
Central African Republic
Chad
Chile
Colombia*
Comoros
Congo
§Costa Rica
Côte d'Ivoire
Cyprus
Djibouti
§Dominica***
§Dominican Republic
Ecuador*
Egypt
§El Salvador
Equatorial Guinea
Fiji
Gambia
Ghana
§Grenada***
§Guatemala
Guinea
Guinea Bissau
§Guyana***
§Haiti
§Honduras
Hungary
India
Indonesia**
Israel
§Jamaica***
Jordan
Kenya
Kiribati
Lebanon
Lesotho
Madagascar
Malawi
Malaysia**
Maldives
Mali
Malta
Mauritania
Maritius
Mexico
Morocco
Mozambique
Namibia
Nepal
Niger
Oman
Pakistan
Papua New Guinea
Paraguay
Peru*
Philippines**
Poland
Rwanda
§Saint Kitts (Christopher) and Nevis
§Saint Lucia***
§Saint Vincent and the Grenadines***
Sao Tome and Principe
Senegal
Seychelles
Sierra Leone
Solomon Islands
Somalia
Sri Lanka
Sudan
Surinam
Swaziland
Syria
Tanzania
Thailand**
Togo
Tonga
§Trinidad and Tobago***
Tunisia
Turkey
Tuvalu
Uganda
Uruguay
Vanuatu
Venezuela*
Western Samoa
Yemen Arab Republic Sanaa
Yugoslavia
Zaire
Zambia
Zimbabwe

*Member countries of the Cartagena Agreement—Andean Group (treated as one country).

**Association of South East Asian Nationals—Nations (ASEAN) except Brunei, Dar es Salaam and Singapore (treated as one country).

***Member countries of the Caribbean Common Market. (CARICOM).

§$600 personal exemption (Panama and Nicaragua are also eligible).

Non-Independent Countries and Territories

Anguilla
§Aruba
British Indian Ocean Territory
Cayman Islands
Christmas Island (Australia)
Cocos (Keeling) Islands
Cook Islands
Falkland Islands (Islas Malvinas)
French Polynesia
Gibraltar
Greenland
Heard Island and McDonald Islands
Macau
§Montserrat*
§Netherlands Antilles
New Caledonia
Niue
Norfolk Island
Pitcairn Islands
Saint Helena
Tokelau
Trust Territory of the Pacific Islands (Palau)
Turks and Caicos Islands
§Virgin Islands, British
Wallis and Futuna
Western Sahara

*Member countries of the Caribbean Common Market (CARICOM).

§ $600 personal exemption (Panama and Nicaragua are also eligible for this exemption).

DEPARTMENT OF THE TREASURY, U.S. CUSTOMS SERVICE, Washington, D.C. 20229. Customs Publication No. 515. Revised February 1991.

Appendix C

COMPARATIVE CLOTHING SIZES U.S./EUROPEAN

Men's Suits

U.S.	34	35	36	37	38	39	40	41	42
Europe	44	46	48	49½	51	52½	54	55½	57

Shirts

U.S.	14½	15	15½	16	16½	17
Europe	37	38	39	41	42	43

Shoes

U.S.	7	8	9	10	11	12	13
Europe	39½	41	42	43	44½	46	47

Hats

U.S.	6⅞	7	7⅛	7¼	7⅜	7½	7⅞
Europe	55	56	57	58	59	60	61

Women's Dresses

U.S.	8	10	12	14	16	18
Europe	38	40	42	44	46	48

Blouses and sweaters

U.S.	10	12	14	16	18	20
Europe	38	40	42	44	46	48

Stockings

U.S.	8	9	9½	10	10½	11
Europe	1	2	3	4	5	6

Shoes

U.S.	4½	5	5½	6	6½	7	7½	8	8½
Europe	35½	36	36½	37	37½	38	38½	39	39½

Gloves

Sizes are usually the same in Europe and the U.S.

Children's Clothes

U.S. (age)	3	4	5	6
Europe (height)	98 cm	104 cm	110 cm	116 cm

Shoes

U.S.	8	9	10	11	12	13	1	2	3	4½
Europe	24	25	27	28	29	30	32	33	34	36

Appendix D

SYMBOLS FOR MONETARY UNITS

	Chinese*	Arabic	Hebrew	Greek (Upper Case)	Greek (Lower Case)	Sanskrit
1	一	١	א	A	ᾱ	१
2	二	٢	ב	B	β̄	२
3	三	٣	ג	Γ	γ̄	३
4	四	٤	ד	Δ	δ̄	४
5	五	٥	ה	E	ε̄	५
6	六	٦	ו	F	ϛ̄	६
7	七	٧	ז	Z	ζ̄	७
8	八	٨	ח	H	η̄	८
9	九	٩	ט	Θ	θ̄	९
10	十	١٠	י	I	ῑ	

*Japanese and Thai symbols are not included here due to their similarity to the Chinese.

Appendix E

LETTERS OF CREDIT

Excerpts from an introduction to and explanation of letters of credit by Leonard Back, Vice President of Citibank, N.A.

Commercial Credits—Advantages to Buyers and Sellers

In a broad sense, a commercial letter of credit, sometimes referred to as a "Credit" or "Commercial Credit," is simply a letter of instructions issued to an exporter by a bank at the request of its customer. In its narrowest sense, it is a specialized and technical instrument used to finance a shipment of goods from one party to another. Whether a Credit is highly specialized or simple is determined usually not by its construction but rather by how well versed its users are in the language and practices of international trade.

Its users in any event rely upon Commercial Credits to finance the purchase of goods or services. International trade historically has involved buyers and sellers striving to conduct trade despite differences in language, national customs, credit procedures, and accounting practices. Such variances have led merchants to seek a protective device to minimize the effects of nationalistic diversities and at the same time to facilitate trade and payments for goods. Commercial Credits are instruments well designed to meet this international need. Within the United States sales and purchases of goods and services between parties are far less complicated than when dealing across international boundaries. The speed and simplicity of communication, of shipment, and of credit arrangements all have served to lessen the domestic dependency on Commercial Letters of Credit as a financing tool. However, whenever U.S. firms need the special protection and opportunities that Commercial Credits offer, such instruments can be equally useful in the domestic market.

Methods of Financing International Trade

An international seller of merchandise has five alternatives for obtaining payment of goods shipped to an overseas buyer.

1. The seller may request cash from the buyer in advance of shipment.

2. There may be an "open account" arrangement whereby the buyer effects payment through some method privately concluded with the seller.

3. The goods may be shipped "on consignment" whereby the buyer received the goods but makes payment to the seller only if and as the goods are sold by the buyer; meanwhile ownership of any unsold goods remains with the shipper.

4. The seller may ship on a collection basis, presenting the documents covering the shipment through the banking system together with a draft (bill of exchange) drawn on the buyer for the value of the shipment. Upon presentation to the buyer of the draft and documents the buyer must honor the draft before the documents covering the shipment are released to him.

5. The seller may request the buyer to establish a Commercial Letter of Credit in favor of the seller for the value of the shipment. It is this type of transaction which will be discussed in detail.

In the first three financing methods the documents covering the export of merchandise would be handled outside banking channels and the banking system would not be involved other than for the international remittances of funds. If financed on a collection basis or a Commercial Letter of Credit basis, however, a bank would participate somewhere in the transaction adding its service and documentary expertise to the buyer and seller, or both.

With several methods of financing available to a buyer and seller of goods, why would a buyer and seller want to use a Commercial Credit to finance a shipment? One simple answer would be that the seller will not ship unless he has a bank's assurance of payment. This is indeed a major factor behind such financing, but there are advantages for the buyer as well as other advantages for the seller which add to the usefulness of Commercial Credit financing.

Advantages to the Buyer

1) The buyer applying to his bank for establishment of a Commercial Credit has the assurance that his bank will refuse any payment to the seller unless the seller has complied with the terms of the Credit, terms which the buyer has given to his bank and which are stipulated in the Commercial Credit.

2) If the buyer arranges for a Commercial Credit which by prior agreement of the seller is payable not upon presentation of documents by the seller but say 60 or 90 days after presentation, the buyer has received credit terms at a cost possibly less than if he found it necessary to borrow funds for 60 or 90 days in order to pay the seller immediately. Later we shall learn why sellers of goods under Commercial Credits may be perfectly willing to grant extended terms for payment, whereas such terms would not be granted if the shipment were financed by other means.

3) It is possible in the U.S. and undoubtedly in many other countries for the buyer under a Commercial Credit, having received and paid for the imported goods, to refinance the goods until they are marketable. One such type of financing subsequently will be covered in detail under the subject of Bankers Acceptance Financing.

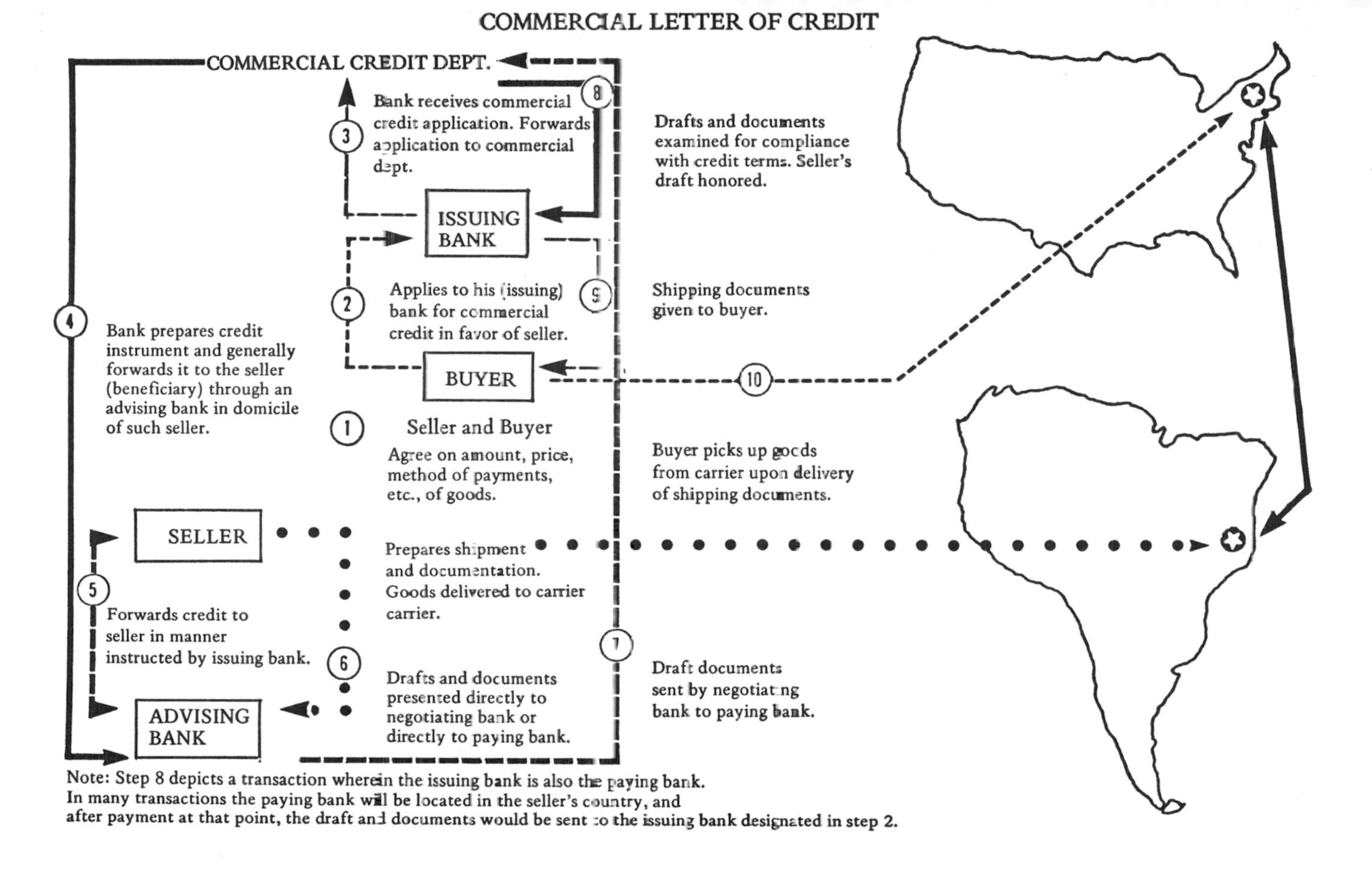
COMMERCIAL LETTER OF CREDIT
COMMERCIAL CREDIT DEPT.
8
Bank receives commercial credit application. Forwards application to commercial dept.
3
Drafts and documents examined for compliance with credit terms. Seller's draft honored.
ISSUING BANK
2
Applies to his (issuing) bank for commercial credit in favor of seller.
9
Shipping documents given to buyer.
4
Bank prepares credit instrument and generally forwards it to the seller (beneficiary) through an advising bank in domicile of such seller.
BUYER
10
1
Seller and Buyer
Agree on amount, price, method of payments, etc., of goods.
Buyer picks up goods from carrier upon delivery of shipping documents.
SELLER
Prepares shipment and documentation. Goods delivered to carrier carrier.
5
Forwards credit to seller in manner instructed by issuing bank.
7
6
Drafts and documents presented directly to negotiating bank or directly to paying bank.
Draft documents sent by negotiating bank to paying bank.
ADVISING BANK
Note: Step 8 depicts a transaction wherein the issuing bank is also the paying bank.
In many transactions the paying bank will be located in the seller's country, and
after payment at that point, the draft and documents would be sent to the issuing bank designated in step 2.

Advantages to the Seller

1) The seller, as previously mentioned, benefits through receiving a Commercial Credit undertaking from a bank. He relies on the credit extended by a bank rather than a credit extended by the merchant.

2) The seller is less apprehensive that payment for his goods might be delayed or otherwise jeopardized by political acts or foreign exchange problems in the buyer's country. Holding a bank's commitment, the seller "feels safe."

3) The existence of Commercial Credit in the exporter's favor may provide the basis whereby the exporter can obtain a loan to purchase or manufacture the goods *prior to shipping* under the Credit. Under Bankers Acceptance financing which will be discussed in a later chapter, the exporter may place himself in funds *shortly after shipment* despite having granted credit terms to the buyer.

Commercial Letters of Credit and Contracts

Sales of merchandise are concluded privately between a buyer and seller (or through their agents) and the agreement of the two parties is evidenced by a contract of sale, whether formally written or orally agreed upon (business wisdom recommends all agreements or contracts should be in writing). As part of the sale agreement or contract, the terms of sale and the method of payment for the goods would be established. If a Commercial Letter of Credit is designated as the financing medium, the buyer would apply to his bank for the issuance of a Commercial Credit in favor of the seller for the purpose of inducing the seller to proceed with the shipment.

The application for Commercial Credit which the buyer makes to his bank introduces another type of contractual agreement, a contract separate and distinct from the contract of sale. This contract is between the buyer, as applicant, and his bank, and sets forth the financial obligation and responsibility of the buyer to the bank in respect to the issuance of the Commercial Credit. The application will doubtless also set forth the terms, provisions and conditions which are to be included in the Commercial Letter of Credit.

The buyer's bank in issuing the Commercial Credit will enter into yet another form of contract, expressed in the terms of the Letter of Credit instrument. For the Commercial Credit instrument itself is a form of contractual obligation of the issuing bank. Although more will be said about irrevocable and revocable instruments, at this point it will suffice to state that Commercial Credits are predominantly issued as irrevocable instruments and, as such, the seller who complies with the terms of the instrument has a contractual commitment of a bank to effect payment. In effect, the bank issuing the commercial credit has substituted its own credit standing for that of the buyer. The seller no longer will rely on (or be concerned about) the willingness or ability of the buyer to make payment for the goods. The bank will undertake to make payment and the seller will look to the bank, not to the buyer for payment.

The Commercial Credit instrument usually will be less detailed than the sales contract and will represent an undertaking by a bank, an undertaking which is not contingent upon whether the seller complied with the terms of the sales contract.

Having briefly described the contractual aspect of Commercial Credits, it is necessary to clarify that our description of a Commercial Credit as a contract may be subject to question by the student of law. In fact, one authority states that "The legal character of a banker's commercial letter of credit is open to almost infinite debate and becomes susceptible to the most scholastic treatment."* However, for the layman it is well to recognize that a Commercial Credit, when irrevocable, does represent a legal commitment by a bank to the seller (beneficiary), *provided the beneficiary has met the terms of the instrument.*

*Wilbert Ward and Henry Harfield, *Bank Credits and Acceptances*, 4th ed. The Ronald Press Company, New York, 1958, p.33.

Now that the Commercial Credit has been discussed as to its legal implication, something should be said briefly about what a Commercial Credit is not intended to accomplish.

1) Its existence is never a guarantee of payment to anyone; in other words, its existence only assures payment to a beneficiary (shipper) if its terms and conditions are fulfilled.

2) The Commercial Credit does not insure that the goods purchased will be those invoiced and shipped. Banks dealing in Commercial Credits deal in documents not in merchandise. The quantity and quality of goods shipped, although possibly specified in the documents submitted to the bank as required by the Credit terms, ultimately depends upon the honesty and integrity of the seller *or* his agent who has manufactured, packaged, cartoned, or crated, and arranged for shipment of the merchandise.

It is possible for the buyer to make provision in a Commercial Credit for verification of quantity and/or quality by requiring that independent testing laboratory certificates or inspection certificates be submitted along with other documents. Since such quantity or quality analysis involves some expense, the buyer and seller should agree beforehand as to how such expenses are to be covered.

The integrity of the buyer and seller, of course, are paramount in any exchange of goods or services no matter what financing medium is used. As a financing medium, Commercial Letters of Credit afford the seller of goods an assured means of financial settlement with protection not usually found in other financing arrangements except by actual cash payment in advance. The buyer, on the other hand, gains the protection that the exporter will not benefit at the buyer's expense, until documentary evidence has been submitted to a bank assuring that the exporter has complied with the buyer's documentary requirements set forth in the commercial credit. These and the other advantages previously mentioned have enabled the use of Commercial Letters of Credit to expand with the growth of international trade, a fact which attests to the reliance by merchants throughout the world on this type of banking instrument for minimizing credit risks while at the same time meeting the financial requirements of the parties.

The Parties to Commercial Credits

Up to this point, three basic parties have been mentioned, the buyer (importer), the seller (exporter), and the bank. In an actual transaction, there will usually be more than one bank participating. At any rate, the various parties to the Credit are described in banking terminology as follows:

The Accountee—This is the buyer-importer or the applicant who arranges for the establishment of the Credit.

The Beneficiary—The party in whose favor the instrument is issued (usually the seller-exporter).

The Opening Bank (Issuing Bank)—The Accountee's (buyer's) bank which issues the Credit.

The Paying Bank—The bank named in the Commercial Credit as the bank which will effect payment to the Beneficiary.

The Advising Bank (Notifying Bank)—The bank who advises or sends the instrument to the Beneficiary. It may be either the Opening Bank, Paying Bank, or yet another bank.

The Negotiating Bank—A bank usually unnamed in the Credit instrument which elects to "negotiate" (advance funds) to the Beneficiary against presentation of the documents required by the Credit terms.

The Confirming Bank—The bank which adds its own irrevocable undertaking that the Opening Bank will fulfill its irrevocable obligation under the Commercial Credit.

A particular bank may play several of the aforementioned roles in a single transaction. If, for example, the Opening Bank issues its instrument directly to the Beneficiary, payable at the bank's own office, that bank is performing the role of Advising Bank and Paying Bank in addition to that of Opening Bank. There are instances, however, where several banks may be involved.

By way of illustration, if the Rhine Bank in Germany (Opening Bank) issues a Commercial Credit payable in U.S. dollars at First National City Bank, New York (Paying Bank) and requests that bank to notify the Beneficiary in Japan, First National City Bank, New York, may forward the instrument to its Tokyo Branch (Advising Bank) who will advise the terms of the Credit to the Beneficiary. The Beneficiary may then choose to present his draft and documents under the Credit to his local Japanese bank for negotiation (Negotiating Bank), if negotiation is otherwise not restricted to a bank named in the instrument.

In most instances there are at least two banks in each transaction, the bank in the buyer's country, and the bank in the seller's country. However, it would not be unusual to find three and sometimes four banks participating in a transaction particularly where shipments between foreign countries are financed in U.S. dollars.

LEARN THE LANGUAGE

Types of Credit Extension

Having become familiar with the participants in Commercial Letters of Credit—the Accountee, Beneficiary, and the banks, it is important to become familiar with the language used by these parties in Commercial Credit transactions.

Irrevocable Vs. Revocable

Earlier the word "irrevocable" was used in describing a type of Commercial Credit transaction. Commercial Credits are issued in either "irrevocable" or "revocable" form. What do these terms mean? Simply stated, an irrevocable Credit cannot be changed without the agreement of all parties. Conversely a revocable Credit can be changed or canceled by the Opening Bank at any time with or *without notice* to the Beneficiary. If a Credit instrument is revocable and designated a bank other than the Opening Bank as the Paying Bank, the Paying Bank will revoke its agreement to pay under the credit upon receipt of a notice of revocation from the Opening Bank provided payment has not been previously effected. Whether the Credit instrument is issued in irrevocable or revocable form will be decided upon by the Accountee, usually in accordance with prior agreement of the Beneficiary-Seller.

In its function the *revocable Credit* is not truly a bank Credit but rather serves as a device which provides the buyer and seller with a means of settling payments for shipments. Since a revocable Credit can be canceled or changed without notice, the Beneficiary of a revocable Credit should not rely on the Credit instrument for credit protection. He must have faith that the buyer will abide by the sales contract or other agreement and will not revoke the revocable Credit.

An *irrevocable Letter of Credit*, however, is a definite undertaking that the Opening Bank will effect payment provided the Beneficiary complies with the terms and conditions stipulated in the Credit instrument. The terms and conditions of an irrevocable Credit cannot be changed without the consent of the Opening Bank, Confirming Bank (if confirmed), and the Beneficiary. The illustration on page 178 depicts an irrevocable credit and it will be noted that First National City Bank, as the Opening Bank, sets forth its engagement or undertaking in the last paragraph of this form. The Beneficiary therefore holds an undertaking not of the Accountee—buyer, but of the Opening Bank, First National City Bank. In the absence of the language shown in the last paragraph of this form, the term "irrevocable" used in the title of the instrument conveys this type of banking obligation.

Confirmed Vs. Unconfirmed

In Commercial Credits, it is important to distinguish which bank gives its irrevocable undertaking. For example, United States banks frequently use their own forms to convey to the Beneficiary the irrevocable undertaking of an overseas Opening Bank. See illustration on page 179. Such instruments bear

irrevocable letter of credit

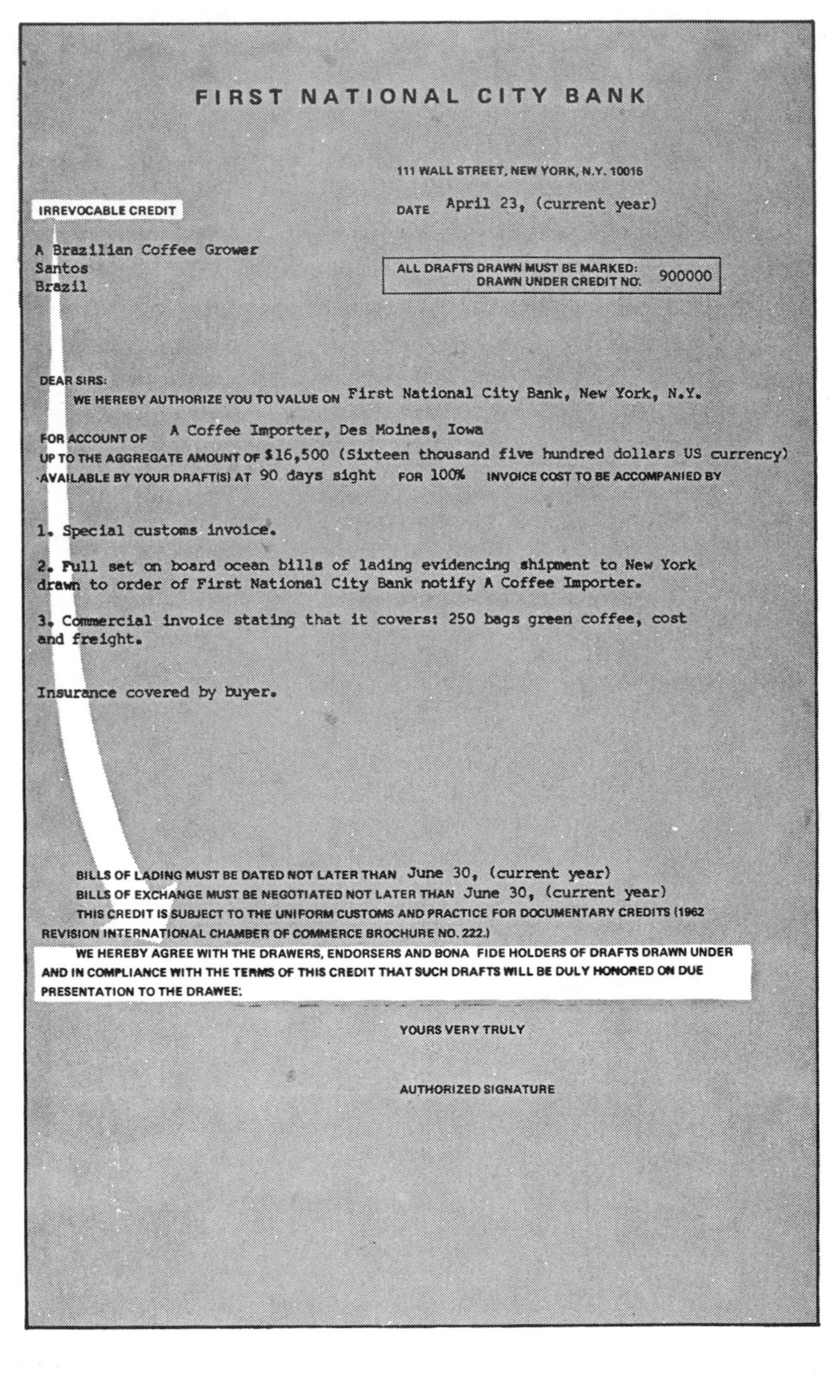

FIRST NATIONAL CITY BANK

111 WALL STREET, NEW YORK, N.Y. 10015

IRREVOCABLE CREDIT

DATE April 23, (current year)

A Brazilian Coffee Grower
Santos
Brazil

ALL DRAFTS DRAWN MUST BE MARKED:
DRAWN UNDER CREDIT NO. 900000

DEAR SIRS:
WE HEREBY AUTHORIZE YOU TO VALUE ON First National City Bank, New York, N.Y.

FOR ACCOUNT OF A Coffee Importer, Des Moines, Iowa
UP TO THE AGGREGATE AMOUNT OF $16,500 (Sixteen thousand five hundred dollars US currency)
AVAILABLE BY YOUR DRAFT(S) AT 90 days sight FOR 100% INVOICE COST TO BE ACCOMPANIED BY

1. Special customs invoice.

2. Full set on board ocean bills of lading evidencing shipment to New York drawn to order of First National City Bank notify A Coffee Importer.

3. Commercial invoice stating that it covers: 250 bags green coffee, cost and freight.

Insurance covered by buyer.

BILLS OF LADING MUST BE DATED NOT LATER THAN June 30, (current year)
BILLS OF EXCHANGE MUST BE NEGOTIATED NOT LATER THAN June 30, (current year)
THIS CREDIT IS SUBJECT TO THE UNIFORM CUSTOMS AND PRACTICE FOR DOCUMENTARY CREDITS (1962 REVISION INTERNATIONAL CHAMBER OF COMMERCE BROCHURE NO. 222.)

WE HEREBY AGREE WITH THE DRAWERS, ENDORSERS AND BONA FIDE HOLDERS OF DRAFTS DRAWN UNDER AND IN COMPLIANCE WITH THE TERMS OF THIS CREDIT THAT SUCH DRAFTS WILL BE DULY HONORED ON DUE PRESENTATION TO THE DRAWEE.

YOURS VERY TRULY

AUTHORIZED SIGNATURE

irrevocable undertaking

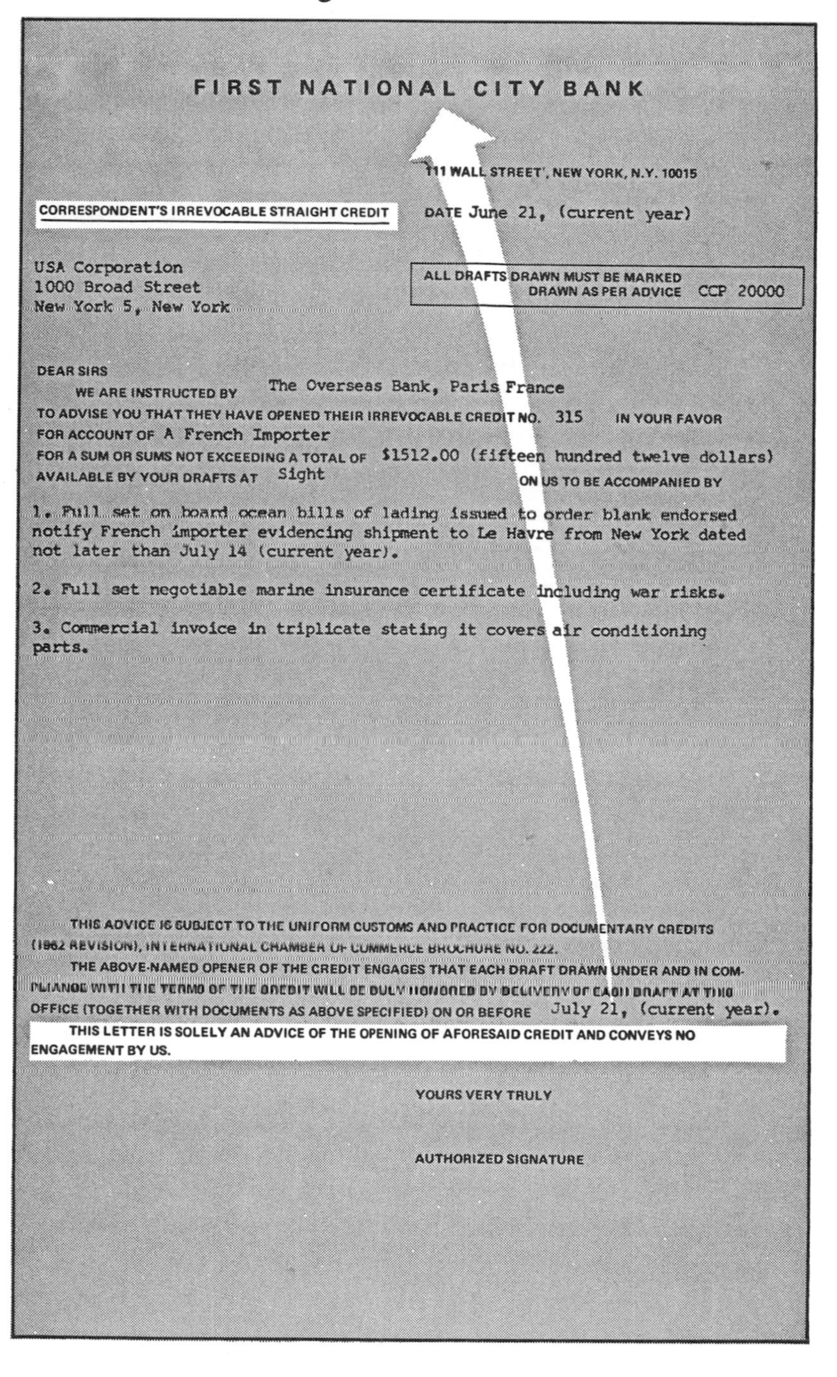

FIRST NATIONAL CITY BANK

111 WALL STREET, NEW YORK, N.Y. 10015

CORRESPONDENT'S IRREVOCABLE STRAIGHT CREDIT

DATE June 21, (current year)

USA Corporation
1000 Broad Street
New York 5, New York

ALL DRAFTS DRAWN MUST BE MARKED
DRAWN AS PER ADVICE CCP 20000

DEAR SIRS

WE ARE INSTRUCTED BY The Overseas Bank, Paris France
TO ADVISE YOU THAT THEY HAVE OPENED THEIR IRREVOCABLE CREDIT NO. 315 IN YOUR FAVOR
FOR ACCOUNT OF A French Importer
FOR A SUM OR SUMS NOT EXCEEDING A TOTAL OF $1512.00 (fifteen hundred twelve dollars)
AVAILABLE BY YOUR DRAFTS AT Sight ON US TO BE ACCOMPANIED BY

1. Full set on board ocean bills of lading issued to order blank endorsed notify French importer evidencing shipment to Le Havre from New York dated not later than July 14 (current year).

2. Full set negotiable marine insurance certificate including war risks.

3. Commercial invoice in triplicate stating it covers air conditioning parts.

THIS ADVICE IS SUBJECT TO THE UNIFORM CUSTOMS AND PRACTICE FOR DOCUMENTARY CREDITS (1962 REVISION), INTERNATIONAL CHAMBER OF COMMERCE BROCHURE NO. 222.

THE ABOVE-NAMED OPENER OF THE CREDIT ENGAGES THAT EACH DRAFT DRAWN UNDER AND IN COMPLIANCE WITH THE TERMS OF THE CREDIT WILL BE DULY HONORED BY DELIVERY OF EACH DRAFT AT THIS OFFICE (TOGETHER WITH DOCUMENTS AS ABOVE SPECIFIED) ON OR BEFORE July 21, (current year).

THIS LETTER IS SOLELY AN ADVICE OF THE OPENING OF AFORESAID CREDIT AND CONVEYS NO ENGAGEMENT BY US.

YOURS VERY TRULY

AUTHORIZED SIGNATURE

the word "irrevocable." However, the legal language must be read to determine the extent of bank commitment. Credits which are irrevocable on the part of the Opening Bank and which are *advised* to the Beneficiary on the instrument of the Paying Bank, will bear a notation by such Paying Bank or Advising Bank that it makes *"no engagement"* or words to that effect. The instrument is therefore, irrevocable on the part of the Opening Bank only, and the Paying Bank acts merely as paying agent of the Opening Bank, not as a party to the irrevocable undertaking. Such instruments may be designated as Correspondent's Irrevocable Credits, such as our illustration, page 182. Beneficiaries of such instruments are dependent upon the creditworthiness of the Opening Bank for fulfillment of its irrevocable undertaking.

Beneficiaries (exporters) are not always willing to rely upon the credit standing of an Opening Bank. This is particularly true when the Bank is in a foreign country and is of unknown standing to the Beneficiary. Consequently, a Beneficiary may request the Accountee-buyer to have the Commercial Credit opened in irrevocable form by a bank in the buyer's country, and confirmed by a bank in the Beneficiary's country. For example, if an Overseas Bank (buyer's bank) opens its irrevocable Credit payable at First National City Bank, New York, and requests First National City Bank to add its confirmation and advise the Credit to the Beneficiary, the First National City Bank, as Paying, Advising, and Confirming Bank, will issue its instrument, an example of which appears on page 183. In the language of this Credit, First National City Bank undertakes to effect payment under the terms and conditions of the Opening Bank's Credit. The Beneficiary, therefore, has a commitment from a Bank in his own country and need not be concerned in general about the ability or willingness of the Overseas Bank to fulfill its engagement.

Before adding its confirmation, the Confirming Bank will satisfy itself that the Credit standing of the Opening Bank justifies confirmation of its irrevocable Credit. This is necessary since a failure of the Overseas Bank to fulfill its obligation through political restraint, war, or insolvency, etc., will not relieve the Confirming Bank of its obligation to the Beneficiary.

FIRST NATIONAL CITY BANK

111 WALL STREET, NEW YORK, N.Y. 10015

CORRESPONDENT'S IRREVOCABLE STRAIGHT CREDIT

DATE June 21, (current year)

USA Corporation
1000 Broad Street
New York 5, New York

ALL DRAFTS DRAWN MUST BE MARKED
DRAWN AS PER ADVICE CCP 20000

DEAR SIRS

WE ARE INSTRUCTED BY The Overseas Bank, Paris France
TO ADVISE YOU THAT THEY HAVE OPENED THEIR IRREVOCABLE CREDIT NO. 315 IN YOUR FAVOR
FOR ACCOUNT OF A French Importer
FOR A SUM OR SUMS NOT EXCEEDING A TOTAL OF $1512.00 (fifteen hundred twelve dollars)
AVAILABLE BY YOUR DRAFTS AT Sight ON US TO BE ACCOMPANIED BY

1. Full set on board ocean bills of lading issued to order blank endorsed notify French importer evidencing shipment to Le Havre from New York dated not later than July 14 (current year).

2. Full set negotiable marine insurance certificate including war risks.

3. Commercial invoice in triplicate stating it covers air conditioning parts.

THIS ADVICE IS SUBJECT TO THE UNIFORM CUSTOMS AND PRACTICE FOR DOCUMENTARY CREDITS (1962 REVISION), INTERNATIONAL CHAMBER OF COMMERCE BROCHURE NO. 222.

THE ABOVE-NAMED OPENER OF THE CREDIT ENGAGES THAT EACH DRAFT DRAWN UNDER AND IN COMPLIANCE WITH THE TERMS OF THE CREDIT WILL BE DULY HONORED BY DELIVERY OF EACH DRAFT AT THIS OFFICE (TOGETHER WITH DOCUMENTS AS ABOVE SPECIFIED) ON OR BEFORE July 21, (current year).

THIS LETTER IS SOLELY AN ADVICE OF THE OPENING OF AFORESAID CREDIT AND CONVEYS NO ENGAGEMENT BY US.

YOURS VERY TRULY

AUTHORIZED SIGNATURE

FIRST NATIONAL CITY BANK

111 WALL STREET, NEW YORK, N.Y. 10015

CONFIRMED IRREVOCABLE STRAIGHT CREDIT

DATE June 21, (current year)

USA Corporation
1000Broad Street
New York, New York 10005

ALL DRAFTS DRAWN MUST BE MARKED: DRAWN AS PER ADVICE CCP 20000

DEAR SIRS:

WE ARE INSTRUCTED BY The Overseas Bank, Paris, France

TO ADVISE YOU THAT IT HAS OPENED ITS IRREVOCABLE CREDIT NO. 315 IN YOUR FAVOR
FOR ACCOUNT OF A French Importer
FOR A SUM OR SUMS NOT EXCEEDING A TOTAL OF $1512.00 (fifteen hundred twelve dollars)
AVAILABLE BY YOUR DRAFTS AT Sight ON US TO BE ACCOMPANIED BY

1. Full set on board ocean bills of lading issued by order blank endorsed notify Frebch importer evidencing shipment to Le Porte from New York dated not later than July 14, (current year).

2. Full set negotiable marine insurance certificate including war risks.

3. Commercial invoice in triplicate stating that it covers air conditioning parts.

THIS ADVICE IS SUBJECT TO THE UNIFORM CUSTOMS AND PRACTICE FOR DOCUMENTARY CREDITS (1962 REVISION), INTERNATIONAL CHAMBER OF COMMERCE BROCHURE NO. 222.

THE ABOVE-NAMED OPENER OF THE CREDIT ENGAGES WITH YOU THAT EACH DRAFT DRAWN UNDER AND IN COMPLIANCE WITH THE TERMS OF THE CREDIT WILL BE DULY HONORED UPON DELVERY AS SPECIFIED IF PRESENTED AT THIS OFFICE ON OR BEFORE July 21, (current year).

WE CONFIRM THE CREDIT AND THEREBY UNDERTAKE TO HONOR EACH DRAFT DRAWN AND PRESENTED AS ABOVE SPECIFIED.

YOURS VERY TRULY

AUTHORIZED SIGNATURE

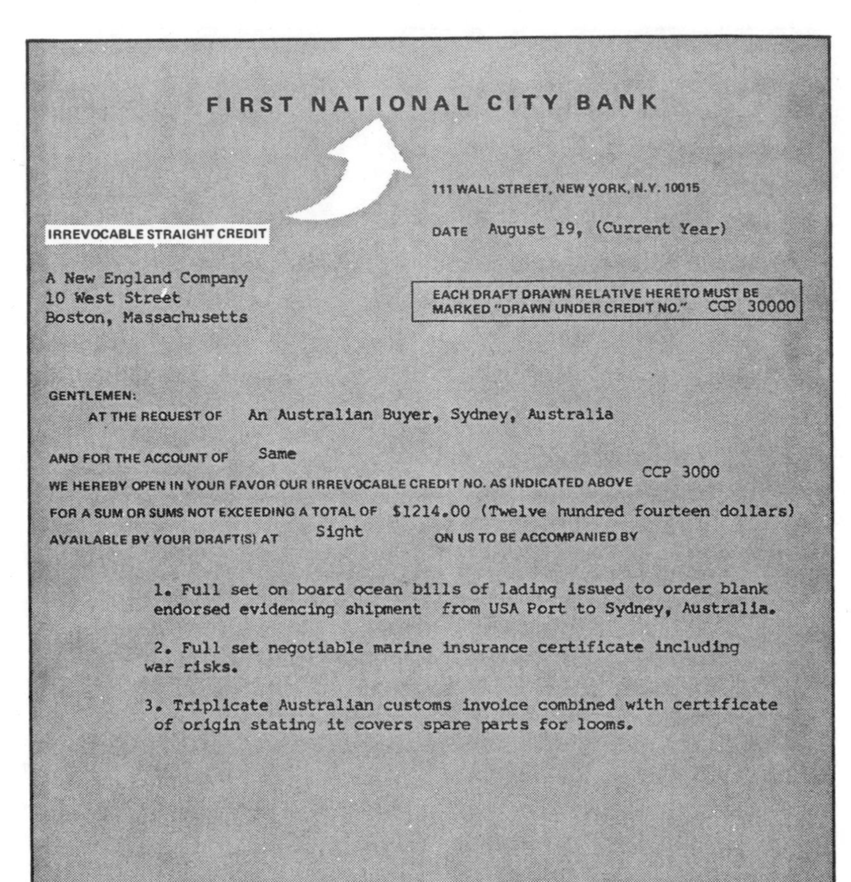
FIRST NATIONAL CITY BANK

111 WALL STREET, NEW YORK, N.Y. 10015

IRREVOCABLE STRAIGHT CREDIT

DATE August 19, (Current Year)

A New England Company
10 West Street
Boston, Massachusetts

EACH DRAFT DRAWN RELATIVE HERETO MUST BE MARKED "DRAWN UNDER CREDIT NO." CCP 30000

GENTLEMEN:

AT THE REQUEST OF An Australian Buyer, Sydney, Australia

AND FOR THE ACCOUNT OF Same

WE HEREBY OPEN IN YOUR FAVOR OUR IRREVOCABLE CREDIT NO. AS INDICATED ABOVE CCP 3000

FOR A SUM OR SUMS NOT EXCEEDING A TOTAL OF $1214.00 (Twelve hundred fourteen dollars)

AVAILABLE BY YOUR DRAFT(S) AT Sight ON US TO BE ACCOMPANIED BY

1. Full set on board ocean bills of lading issued to order blank endorsed evidencing shipment from USA Port to Sydney, Australia.

2. Full set negotiable marine insurance certificate including war risks.

3. Triplicate Australian customs invoice combined with certificate of origin stating it covers spare parts for looms.

THIS CREDIT IS SUBJECT TO THE UNIFORM CUSTOMS AND PRACTICE FOR DOCUMENTARY CREDITS (1962 REVISION INTERNATIONAL CHAMBER OF COMMERCE BROCHURE NO. 222.)

WE HEREBY AGREE TO HONOR EACH DRAFT DRAWN UNDER AND IN COMPLIANCE WITH THE TERMS OF THIS CREDIT, IF DULY PRESENTED (TOGETHER WITH THE DOCUMENTS AS SPECIFIED) AT THIS OFFICE ON OR BEFORE October 15, (Current Year)

VERY TRULY YOURS

AUTHORIZED SIGNATURE

Types of Credit Instruments

In addition to learning the formal language of Commercial Credits, it is equally important to recognize variations in the types of instruments used.

Letter of Credit Conditions

Before leaving the subject of language, it is important to define some of the more common terms and conditions used in Commercial Credit transactions. The terms presented below are basic to most transactions and should be generally understood by those dealing in Commercial Letters of Credit. Credits often contain terms and conditions which are not common, particularly when the instrument is "custom tailored" by the Opening Bank to fit a given customer's needs. However, the following terms and conditions are universally used.

The Tenor. Credit instruments usually require the Beneficiary to draw a draft on the Paying Bank when presenting documents under the Credit. The term of such draft is known as its tenor. If the draft is to be payable upon presentation of the documents or shortly thereafter, the draft required will be drawn payable "at sight" (the tenor). If payable on a term (time) basis, the tenor of the draft may be, for example, 30 days after sight (presentation) or 30 days after date (date of the draft). Although term drafts may be drawn for any number of days, terms are usually in 30 day increments, i.e. 30, 60, 90, 120 days, etc. If a term draft for example is drawn 30 days after sight, the 30 days begin from the date the Paying Bank "accepts" the draft. If 30 days after date, the 30 days run from the date of the draft. When drafts are accepted by a U.S. Paying Bank they take on special properties which will be discussed under the heading of Bankers Acceptance Financing.

The Expiration Date. Commercial Credits expire on stipulated dates. All irrevocable Credits contain an expiration date. If a Revocable Credit instrument fails to contain an expiration date, it will expire automatically six months from date of the notification sent to the Beneficiary. The Beneficiary is required to present the draft and documents to the Paying Bank (or Negotiating Bank for negotiation-type Credits) on or before the date of expiration shown in the instrument. Expiration dates falling on days on which banks are closed for business, become extended to the next business day.

Credits also expire at given locations. Credits issued in negotiation form, i.e. "Irrevocable Negotiation Credit," *expire where negotiated.* Straight Credits, expire *at the office of the Paying Bank.*

Latest Shipping Date. Frequently a Credit instrument states a latest shipping date. The Beneficiary is thus advised that the documents of the carrying steamer, airline, or other designated carrier may not be dated after that date. When "on board" bills of lading are required, the "on board" date is the date of shipment.

If a Beneficiary is unable to meet a stipulated expiration date or a latest shipping date, he should contact the buyer and request an amendment to the Credit to provide a later date for shipment, for expiration, or for both.

On Board. When Credit terms call for steamship "on board" bills of lading, loading "on board" may be evidenced by a bill of lading issued in "on board" form or by a bill of lading bearing an "on board" notation. Such notation (sometimes a super-imposed stamp) must be dated and signed by the carrier. This date cannot be later than the "latest shipping date" shown in the Credit instrument. It is the "on board" date, not the issued date of the bill of lading, which is considered to be the shipping date on steamer shipments.

Unless the Credit terms specify otherwise, failure by the Beneficiary to provide an "on board" bill of lading or to have the steamship company add or affix the "on board" notation on its bill of lading will cause the documents to lack conformity with the Credit terms.

Any term and condition in a Commercial Credit may be amended. If the Accountee requests the Opening Bank to do so and if the Credit is irrevocable, such amendment must always have the Beneficiary's consent. In other words, the Beneficiary may refuse any amendment to an irrevocable Credit at his option. If the Credit is confirmed, the Confirming Bank must also consent to the amendment before the Beneficiary can be advised.

Import Credit

Page 188 illustrates an import transaction. In this case First National City Bank, New York (Citibank) is both Opening Bank, having issued the Credit for the U.S. buyer, and is also the Paying Bank. In possession of an instrument issued by a bank of international reputation, the Japanese Beneficiary-exporter may have his draft under the Credit negotiated at a Japanese bank, thereby placing him in funds shortly after giving up the documents. The Japanese Negotiating Bank will forward the exporter's draft and documents directly to First National City Bank, New York, or through another bank for collection. If the documents conform, "Citibank" will charge its customer, the Accountee-buyer, for the value of the Japanese exporter's draft giving the buyer the documents and simultaneously will make payment to the Japanese Negotiating Bank. If the documents do not conform, "Citibank" will contact its customer, requesting approval of those specifics which do not agree with the terms and conditions of the Credit. If approval is granted, payment will be made. If the importer does not agree, notice will be given to the Japanese Negotiating Bank to that effect requesting their instructions and advising that meanwhile the documents are being held at their disposal.

Bankers Acceptance Financing

Most of the previous discussion dealt with transactions at "sight" whereby the bank makes "payment" under a Commercial Letter of Credit. Indeed the ultimate objective of the Bene-

import credit

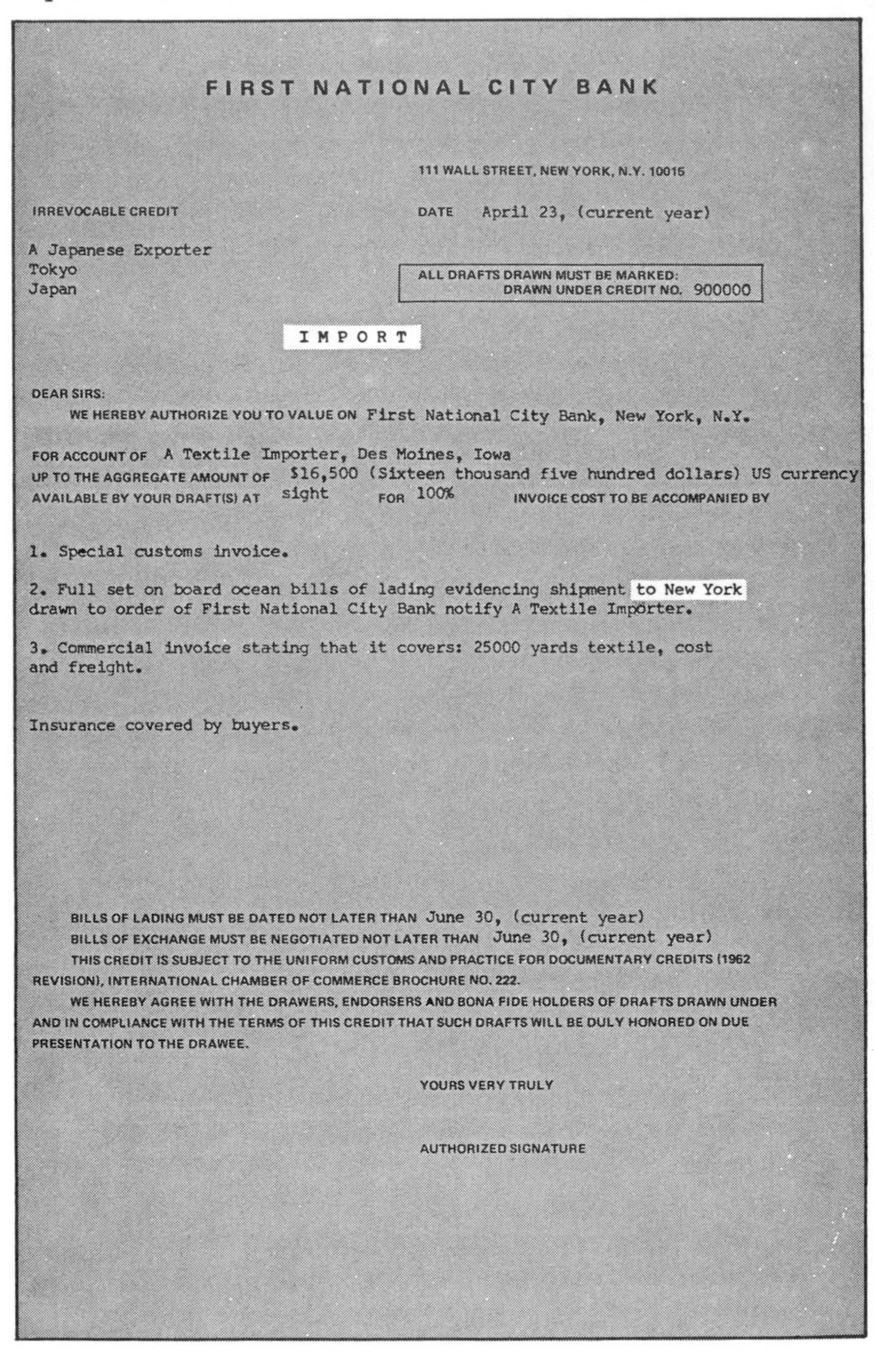

FIRST NATIONAL CITY BANK

111 WALL STREET, NEW YORK, N.Y. 10015

IRREVOCABLE CREDIT

DATE April 23, (current year)

A Japanese Exporter
Tokyo
Japan

ALL DRAFTS DRAWN MUST BE MARKED:
DRAWN UNDER CREDIT NO. 900000

IMPORT

DEAR SIRS:

WE HEREBY AUTHORIZE YOU TO VALUE ON First National City Bank, New York, N.Y.

FOR ACCOUNT OF A Textile Importer, Des Moines, Iowa
UP TO THE AGGREGATE AMOUNT OF $16,500 (Sixteen thousand five hundred dollars) US currency
AVAILABLE BY YOUR DRAFT(S) AT sight FOR 100% INVOICE COST TO BE ACCOMPANIED BY

1. Special customs invoice.

2. Full set on board ocean bills of lading evidencing shipment to New York drawn to order of First National City Bank notify A Textile Importer.

3. Commercial invoice stating that it covers: 25000 yards textile, cost and freight.

Insurance covered by buyers.

BILLS OF LADING MUST BE DATED NOT LATER THAN June 30, (current year)
BILLS OF EXCHANGE MUST BE NEGOTIATED NOT LATER THAN June 30, (current year)
THIS CREDIT IS SUBJECT TO THE UNIFORM CUSTOMS AND PRACTICE FOR DOCUMENTARY CREDITS (1962 REVISION), INTERNATIONAL CHAMBER OF COMMERCE BROCHURE NO. 222.
WE HEREBY AGREE WITH THE DRAWERS, ENDORSERS AND BONA FIDE HOLDERS OF DRAFTS DRAWN UNDER AND IN COMPLIANCE WITH THE TERMS OF THIS CREDIT THAT SUCH DRAFTS WILL BE DULY HONORED ON DUE PRESENTATION TO THE DRAWEE.

YOURS VERY TRULY

AUTHORIZED SIGNATURE

ficiary is to receive payment from the bank which negotiates or pays the draft drawn under the Credit. However, drafts under Letters of Credit also may be drawn on a bank on a time basis, that is, 30, 60 days, etc., after sight or after date. Such drafts are "accepted" upon presentation rather than paid.

When the Beneficiary-exporter of a Commercial Credit has agreed with the buyer for a Credit calling for a draft available at, say, 60 days after sight, the Beneficiary-seller in effect is granting terms to the Accountee-buyer. Thus, when the Beneficiary presents his draft and documents to the Paying Bank under such a condition, he does not expect to receive payment at sight but instead expects the Paying Bank to "accept" his draft to become payable 60 days later. Such a draft drawn in U.S. dollars on and accepted by a prime U.S. bank becomes known as a Bankers Acceptance, a negotiable instrument which the Beneficiary or any other subsequent holder for value may, if he chooses, sell immediately in the Bankers Acceptance market at the current discount rate for such instruments. The Beneficiary, therefore, although granting terms to the buyer, can obtain immediate funds at a discount through sale of his draft accepted by the bank.

Because of the marketable nature of these instruments, Bankers Acceptances, arising from Commercial Credit transactions, offer the exporter or the importer unique opportunity for financing goods on terms which are competitive with other forms of borrowing. Banks which place their "acceptance" on drafts, however, are subject to Federal Reserve Bank regulations governing the use of such instruments. It is useful for all parties to understand the opportunities and limitations relating to Bankers Acceptances as contained in the Federal Reserve Bank regulations.

Generally speaking, a U.S. bank will issue, advise, or confirm a Commercial Credit providing for a draft drawn on itself on a term basis, only if the term of that acceptance is not greater than the period during which the related goods will remain in the channels of trade and in no instance for more than six months (regulations provide for a maximum maturity of six months). For example, a shipment of a perishable commodity from London to New York might be expected to be in the channels of trade for a term of, say 30 days, whereas a shipment from India to Kansas City, Missouri, of durable goods may require an acceptance for a period of 180 days since this type of commodity may remain in the channels of trade for a much longer period. The actual term of the draft would be agreed upon between the buyer and seller and the buyer-applicant would request his bank to issue its Commercial Credit for such terms. The bank's willingness to issue a Credit calling for a term draft would depend upon the credit reliability of its customer, the buyer, and the overall conformity of the transaction within the scope of Federal Reserve Bank Regulations.

Importations to the U.S.

A Commercial Letter of Credit, as illustrated on page 163, provides the overseas coffee exporter the same opportunity to extend credit terms to the U.S. importer and to arrange for the discount of an acceptance, as our previous illustration of an export from the U.S. Bankers Acceptances in U.S. dollars affords the overseas Beneficiary the means for having the acceptance discounted in the U.S., thereby placing the Beneficiary in funds immediately, whereas the U.S. importer will be required to make payment only at maturity of the acceptance. The cost of discounting at the market rate for Bankers Acceptances will be borne by the overseas Beneficiary unless provision has been made in the Credit terms for payment of such discount by the U.S. applicant for the Credit (Accountee). [insert graphic]

commercial letter of credit

FIRST NATIONAL CITY BANK

111 WALL STREET, NEW YORK, N.Y. 10015

IRREVOCABLE CREDIT

DATE April 23 (current year)

A Brazilian Coffee Grower
Santos
Brazil

ALL DRAFTS DRAWN MUST BE MARKED:
DRAWN UNDER CREDIT NO. 900000

Import Credit - Import Financing

DEAR SIRS:

WE HEREBY AUTHORIZE YOU TO VALUE ON First National City Bank, New York, N.Y.
FOR ACCOUNT OF A Coffee Importer, Des Moines, Iowa
UP TO THE AGGREGATE AMOUNT OF $16,500(Sixteen thousand five hundred dollars U.S. currency)
AVAILABLE BY YOUR DRAFT(S) AT 90 days sight FOR 100% INVOICE COST TO BE ACCOMPANIED BY

1. Special customs invoice.

2. Full set on board ocean bills of lading evidencing shipment to New York drawn to order of First National City Bank notify A Coffee Importer.

3. Commercial invoice stating that it covers: 250 bags green coffee, cost and freight

Insurance covered by buyer.

BILLS OF LADING MUST BE DATED NOT LATER THAN June 30, (current year)
BILLS OF EXCHANGE MUST BE NEGOTIATED NOT LATER THAN June 30, (current year)
THIS CREDIT IS SUBJECT TO THE UNIFORM CUSTOMS AND PRACTICE FOR DOCUMENTARY CREDITS (1962 REVISION INTERNATIONAL CHAMBER OF COMMERCE BROCHURE NO. 222.)

WE HEREBY AGREE WITH THE DRAWERS, ENDORSERS AND BONA FIDE HOLDERS OF DRAFTS DRAWN UNDER AND IN COMPLIANCE WITH THE TERMS OF THIS CREDIT THAT SUCH DRAFTS WILL BE DULY HONORED ON DUE PRESENTATION TO THE DRAWEE.

YOURS VERY TRULY

AUTHORIZED SIGNATURE

TERMS USED IN FOREIGN TRADE

The terms used below are not all of the terms used in foreign trade, but they are some of those most frequently encountered. This is not meant to be the legal definitions of words, but the definitions that are generally understood and used in business.

a.a.r.: Against all risks.

A/C: Account.

ACCEPTANCE: Draft which drawee has agreed to pay at a future date.

Bankers Acceptance: draft drawn on a bank and bearing the bank's promise to pay at a future date.

Eligible Bankers Acceptance: one which meets requirements for discounting at a Federal Reserve Bank.

Trade Acceptance: draft drawn on a merchant other than a bank and that merchant's promise to pay at a future date.

AD VALOREM: (Meaning: according to value–from the Latin.) The term is most usually used to describe a method of customs computation, i.e., based on value of product as imported, thus it is often all the cost of a product or commodity including the cost of the goods, insurance, transportation, etc., until it reaches the point of receipt at the port of import in the importing country. A duty is then levied upon this total expense and is figured as a percent of the total amount. (An important exception to this rule is the United States where the Ad Valorem value is figured at the part of export in the country of origin.)

AFTER DATE: Relates to maturity dates of drafts—the time begins to run from the date of a draft bearing the phrase; the fixed date of maturity does not depend upon the date of acceptance of the draft. Compare with After Sight.

AFTER SIGHT: Relates to maturity dates on drafts—time begins to run from the date of acceptance of a draft bearing this phrase. Compare with After Date.

ALLENGE: A slip of paper attached to a bill of exchange, acceptance or note, providing space for additional endorsements.

A/O: Account of.

AT SIGHT: An at sight draft is a draft or bill of exchange to be paid upon presentation or demand.

AUTHORITY TO PAY: Authority to pay is an instruction from a buyer sent from the buyer's bank to the seller's bank, authorizing the seller's bank to pay the seller's draft (or bills of exchange) up to a fixed amount. An authority to pay is usually not confirmed by the seller's local bank, and a seller has no protection against cancelation or modification of an authority to pay.

AWB: Air waybill.

BACK-TO-BACK LETTER OF CREDIT: A term used to denote a form of a letter of credit issued for the account of a buyer of merchandise already holding a favorable letter of credit. The "back-to-back" letter of credit is issued in favor of the supplier of the merchandise to cover the same shipment and subject to similar terms stipulated in the credit already held by the buyer. The terms of both letters of credit, with the exception of the amount and expiration date, are so similar that the same documents presented under the "back-to-back" credit are subsequently applied against the credit in favor of the buyer. However, the buyer or beneficiary of the first credit substitute their draft and invoice for those presented by the supplier.

BANKS: Institutions usually distinguished by the power to take deposits and to make loans.

Central Bank: is the official national bank of a country through which often pass all international import and export transactions and all money exchange. It also sets bank rates of exchange, usually the same as the official rate of exchange. Some central banks delegate those powers specifically to certain nongovernmental banks while in other countries all banks have such power unless otherwise provided.

Correspondent Bank: a depository for another bank. The correspondent bank provides banking services for its depositor within the area or country where the correspondent bank is located.

bbl.: Barrel.

b/d: Barrels per day.

B/D: Bank Draft.

B/E: Bill of exchange.

BENEFICIARY: Party in whose favor a letter of credit is established.

BILL OF EXCHANGE (OR DRAFT): An unconditional written order addressed by one person (drawer) to another (drawee) signed by the drawer and requiring the addressee to pay on demand or at a fixed date a certain sum in money of the order of a specified person (payee), usually the drawer.

BILL OF LADING (OCEAN): A document signed by the captain, agents or owners of a vessel furnishing written evidence of the delivery of merchandise to a destination for seaborne carriage. It represents a receipt for merchandise and contract to deliver it as freight.

Clean: a term describing a bill of lading when the transportation company has not noted irregularities in the packing or general condition of the shipment.

Straight: a nonnegotiable bill of lading that consigns the goods directly to a stipulated consignee.

On Board: a bill of lading only issued when the goods have been placed upon or aboard the specific carrying vehicle (ship, plane, etc.).

On Deck: a bill of lading indicating that the commodity shipped is carried on deck.

Order: a bill of lading usually issued to the shipper, whose endorsement is required to effect its negotiation.

Order "Notify": a bill of lading issued to the order of the shipper with the additional clause that the consignee is to be notified upon arrival of the merchandise, however, without giving the consignee title to the merchandise.

Through Bill of Lading: a bill of lading used when several carriers, normally connecting, are involved.

B/L: Bill of lading

BLOCKED EXCHANGE: Exchange not freely convertible into other currencies.

B.M.: Board measure.

BONDED WAREHOUSE: A building for storing goods authorized by customs officials until removal without the payment of duties.

B/P: Bills payable.

CAD: Cash against documents.

CARRYING COSTS: The cost of warehouse charges, insurance, interest charges, other incidentals, and estimated loss (or gain) in weight.

CASH LETTER OF CREDIT: When the sum indicated on the letter of credit is equal to a sum deposited by the buyer in the issuing bank before the letter is issued, the letter is then known as a cash letter of credit.

C & D: Collected and delivered.

CERTIFICATE OF INSPECTION: A document often required with shipments of perishable or other goods, which certification notes the good condition of the merchandise immediately prior to shipment.

CERTIFICATE OF MANUFACTURE: A certificate of manufacture attests to the manufacturer of a particular good and indicates that it is a good quality and meets the specifications as required.

CERTIFICATE OF ORIGIN: A certificate of origin is issued by the proper authority in the exporting country; it certifies that the origin of the material and the labor used to manufacture those materials are from a specific country and are ready to be exported. Its function is to obtain preferential tariff rates which are available under certain trade agreements between countries.

c.f.: Cubic foot.

C & F: Cost and freight required to ship actual commodities. Same as C.I.F. (which see) except that insurance is arranged by buyer.

CHARGES FORWARD: A banking term used when foreign and domestic bank commission charges, interest and government taxes in connection with the collection of a draft are for the drawee's account.

CHARGES HERE: A banking term used when foreign and domestic bank commission charges, interest and government taxes in connection with the collection of a draft are for the drawer's account.

c.i.: Cost and insurance.

C.I.F.: Cost, insurance and freight required to ship an actual commodity to a point of destination. If a price is quoted C.I.F. this normally means that the seller must pay all of these costs to get the commodity to the point of destination.

C.I.F.E.: Cost, insurance, freight and exchange.

C.I.F.C.: Cost, insurance, freight, and commission.

CLEAN DRAFT: Clean draft is one to which nothing is attached; opposite of a documentary draft.

C.O.D.: Cash on delivery.

COMMERCIAL INVOICE: Bill rendered by exporter for goods shipped; it is one of documents normally accompanying an export draft.

COMMERCIAL PAPER: In international trade (as distinguished from customary usage in domestic finance), any draft or other item to be presented for collection.

COMMERCIAL RATE OF EXCHANGE: The rate of exchange quoted local merchants to exchange local currency for foreign currency offered for payment of locally purchased goods or services.

COMMISSION: The fees charged for handling trade.

COMPOUND DUTY: In customs law, a method of charging duty combining specific and ad valorem duties.

CONFERENCE RATES: Uniform rates established between common ocean carriers operating in the same defined ocean trade area. They are like rates for like products for transport between like points of shipment.

CONFIRMED LETTER OF CREDIT: When a letter of credit is issued by a foreign bank to which a domestic bank adds its confirmation, it becomes known as a confirmed letter of credit. The purpose of this confirmation is to add some responsibility of a domestic bank in the seller's country and to which they have cash access because the issuing bank may be unknown to the seller.

CONTAINER LOAD: A load of commodity or goods on a container.

CONTRACT: A legal arrangement between two parties, whereby each undertakes something to the other. In trade, one party often agrees to provide certain goods at certain terms for the other party, and the second party agrees to pay specified sums on certain terms to the first party. Contracts between buyers and seller are usually in writing or memorialized by written confirmations.

C/P: Customs of the port.

C.R.: Carrier's risk.

CREDIT: Term used interchangeably with letter of credit.

c/s.: Case.

CURRENCY: Something that is in circulation as a medium of exchange—coins, bank and government notes, etc. The exchange value of a currency is what can be obtained with that currency, usually described in terms of another currency such as the exchange value of a dollar in terms of yen.

Devaluating currency: is a currency which has its officially recognized exchange value in terms of some other currency or standard reduced in a formal fashion. Devaluation is a step taken by the government of the country whose currency is at issue. The effect of devaluation is to place the country in a more favorable position with regard to international trade because foreign buyers can obtain more of that country's products for less of their own currency and so are encouraged to buy more.

Hard currency: is a very stable currency, which often is convertible into gold.

Reevaluating currency: a currency which has its exchange value (for another currency) increased by raising its gold equivalency.

Soft currency: a currency subject to possible or frequent devaluations.

Stable currency: a firm currency, relatively unaffected by currency fluctuations and against which softer currencies are often compared.

Weak currency: used interchangeably with soft currency.

C.W.O.: Cash (or check) with order.

D/A: Documents against acceptance; an instruction given for presentation of time drafts, denoting that accompanying documents are to be released on acceptance of draft by drawee.

DATE DRAFT: A draft drawn to mature on a fixed date, irrespective of its acceptance date.

d/b/a: Doing business as.

D/d: Days after date.

D/D: Demand draft.

DEMURRAGE: The charge for delay in unloading a vessel or rail car or for delay in removing merchandise from dock.

Dft.: Draft.

DOCUMENTARY CREDIT: A commercial letter of credit providing for payment by a bank to the named beneficiary, usually the seller of merchandise, against delivery of documents specified in the credit.

DOCUMENTARY DRAFT: A documentary draft is a draft having attached documents that control title to the merchandise for which the draft or bill is presented. The documents are turned over to the drawee when accepted or the accompanying draft is paid.

DOMICILE: The place where a draft or acceptance is made payable.

D/P: Documents against payment; an instruction given for presentation of sight documentary drafts, denoting that accompanying documents are to be released on payment of draft.

DRAFT: An unconditional order for the payment of money drawn by one person (drawer) on another person or bank (drawee) for payment of a specified sum at a fixed date or date determinable in the future, to the benefit of the drawer (beneficiary). The acceptance of a draft occurs after the drawee receives the draft and writes "accepted" over the signature on the draft, together with the date and place of payment at which point the drawee becomes the acceptor and the acceptance occurs. The original copy of the draft when two or more are drawn is called a first of exchange draft. A sight is a draft payable at sight, i.e., when presented for payment. A usance draft is one which is payable at a specified period after sight.

D/S: Days after sight.

DUNNAGE: Loose material used around a cargo to prevent its damage.

DUTY: The customs excise which is calculated generally in two ways:

Ad Valorem duty: essentially, according to value (see Ad Valorem).

Specific duty: an assessment on the weight or quantity of an article without reference to its monetary value or market price.

D/y: Delivery.

E & O.E.: Errors and omissions excepted; a phrase accompanying the shipper's signature on an invoice, by which final responsibility for typographical errors or unintentional omissions is disclaimed.

E.O.M.: End of month.

Est. wt.: Estimated weight.

E.T.A.: Estimated time of arrival.

Ex (POINT OF ORIGIN, such as EX-FACTORY, EX-MILL, EX-WAREHOUSE, EX-DOCK): When a seller quotes a price "Ex" (point), the seller is proposing only to make the merchandise available at that "Ex" point and includes no transportation costs in the quoted prices. The quoted price also would not include any export permit fees, export duties, or other costs of exportation.

Ex/Int.: Not including interest.

EXCHANGE CONTROLS: These are the controls on money placed by a government on the exportation of their own funds or other people's funds out of their country.

Exp.: Export, exported, exporter.

EXPIRATION DATE: The final date upon which drafts under a letter of credit may be presented for negotiations—sometimes also called "expiry."

EX-STORE: Selling term for commodities in warehouse.

F.a.q.: Fair average quality.

F.A.S.: Free alongside ship a price quotation under which the exporter quotes a price that includes delivery of the goods to the vessel's side and within reach of its loading tackle. Subsequent risks and expenses are for the account of the buyer.

F/d: Free at dock.

F & D: Freight and demurrage.

F.f.a.: Free from alongside.

F.O.B.: Free on board; this specifies that the commodity which is being shipped will be placed on the shipping vehicle at no cost to the purchaser, but thereafter the purchaser will bear all costs associated with shipping that commodity.

F.O.C.: Free of charge(s).

F.o.r.: Free on rails at point of destination.

FORCE MAJEURE: A superior or irresistible force beyond the control of the seller and preventing the seller from performing. When stated in a contract, it provides the basis for the seller to make later delivery not strictly pursuant to the terms of the contract because of forces beyond the seller's control.

FORWARD EXCHANGE: Currency bought or sold for delivery at a future time.

F.o.s.: Free on steamer.

F.o.t.: Free on truck.

FREE PORT: Port where merchandise may be stored duty free while awaiting reshipment or while on consignment awaiting sale.

FREE TRADE ZONE: Specific area, in or near a port, offering duty-free storage on same basis as a free port (see above).

frt.: Freight.

fwd.: Forward.

G.A.: General average.

GODOWN: A warehouse in the Far East where goods are stored and delivered when warranted.

GRADING CERTIFICATES: Certificates attesting to quality of a commodity graded by official inspectors, testers, graders, etc.

H: Harbor.

hgt.: Height.

Imp.: Import, imported.

IMPORT CERTIFICATE: A certificate provided by a buyer to a seller certifying the goods being purchased will be imported into the designated country and not reexported to any other country.

IMPORT LICENSE: An import license is granted by the government of an importing country permitting an importer or buyer to import the merchandise described in the import license.

IN BOND: A term applied to the status of merchandise admitted provisionally to a country without payment of duties—either for storage in a bonded warehouse or for trans-shipment to another point, where duties will eventually be imposed.

Ince.: Insurance.

INHERENT VICE: A condition causing damage to merchandise by reason of its own inherent defects.

Inv.: Invoice.

J.A.: Joint account.

k: Kilogram.

K.D.: Knocked down.

L/C: Letter of credit.

ldg.: Loading, landing.

LETTER OF CREDIT: See Appendix E.

M/D: Months after date.

mdse: Merchandise.

MEASUREMENT TON: The measurement ton (also known as the cargo ton or freight ton) is a space measurement, usually 40 cubic feet or one cubic meter. The cargo is assessed a certain rate for every 40 cubic feet of space it occupies.

MT: Metric ton.

NA: Not available.

n.e.i.: Not elsewhere included.

n.e.s.: Not elsewhere specified.

N/F: No funds.

N.O.E.: Not otherwise enumerated.

O/a: On account.

O/c: Open charter.

OCEAN MARINE INSURANCE POLICY: An indemnity contract designed to reimburse an insured for the loss because of unforeseen circumstances or damage to merchandise shipped. The basic marine policy insures transportation perils but can be amended to cover additional hazards.

Open Policy: a marine insurance contract in which the insurer agrees that all shipments moving at the insured's risk are automatically covered under the policy and the insured agrees to report the shipments and to pay premium thereon to the insurer.

Special Marine Policy: sometimes referred to as a marine insurance certificate; this is a policy covering a specific shipment, most frequently used to provide evidence of insurance.

Marine Insurance Terms:

Average: a term of marine insurance meaning loss or damage.

General Average: a loss arising from a voluntary sacrifice made of any part of the vessel or cargo, or expenditure to prevent loss of the whole and for the benefit of all persons at interest. The loss is apportioned among all the shippers including those whose property is lost, and also to the vessel itself. Until the assessment is paid, a lien lies against the entire cargo.

Particular Average: a marine insurance term meaning a partial loss or damage.

With Average (W.A.) or With Particular Average (W.P.A.): provides protection for partial loss by perils of the sea if it amounts to a certain percentage, usually three percent (3%) of the insured value. The 3 percent, a franchise, is not a deductible percentage, rather the minimum amount of claim. The franchise does not apply when a vessel is involved in a fire, stranding, sinking, burning or a collision, or in General Average losses.

Free of Particular Average, American Conditions (F.P.A.A.C.): this covers only those losses directly resulting from fire, stranding, sinking or collision of the vessel.

Free of Particular Average, English Conditions (F.P.A.E.C.): this resembles F.P.A.A.C. except that partial loss resulting from any peril of the sea becomes recoverable when the vessel has been stranded, sunk, burned, on fire or in a collision with the insured cargo aboard. The actual damage need not directly result from these specified perils—only that one of them has occurred.

The foregoing clauses may be broadened by adding coverage for theft, pilferage, nondelivery, breakage, or for example:

All Risks: the broadest marine insurance coverage insures merchandise against all risks of physical loss or damage from any external cause which may arise. Delay, deterioration, loss of market, inherent vice, capture and seizure, war, strikes, riots, and civil commotions represent various exclusions.

Warehouse to Warehouse: a common marine insurance term referring to coverage which attaches to the goods upon their leaving the shipper's warehouse. It continues during the ordinary course of transit until delivery of the merchandise at the consignee's warehouse, within specified time limits.

Both-to-Blame Clause: this constitutes protection against a disclaimer of liability which appears in some bills of lading and purports to operate when damage results from negligence of both vessels that are parties to an accident.

Riots and Civil Commotions (r. & c.c.): the marine policy does not cover the risks of riots and civil commotions except on endorsement.

Free of Capture and Seizure (F.C. & S.): this clause excludes the risks of war and warlike operations from the marine policy.

War Risks: although not covered under any of the foregoing terms of average, the risks of war may be covered under a separate open War Risk Only Policy or by endorsement of the Special or Individual Marine Policy.

OFFICIAL RATE OF EXCHANGE: The official rate of exchange is the rate of exchange established by a government for the currency of that country.

O/o: Order of.

OPEN ACCOUNT: Method of settling an export transaction without use of letters of credit or negotiable instruments evidencing obligation to pay.

O.R.: Owner's risk.

O.R.B.: Owner's risk of breakage.

p.: Per.

p.a.: Per annum.

P.A.: Particular average.

p.c.: Percent.

pcs.: Pieces.

PERILS OF THE SEA: A marine insurance policy phrase referring to accidents or casualties of the sea against which a simple marine policy insures.

p.f.: Pro forma.

P & I: Property and indemnity.

P.L.: Partial loss.

POC: Port of call.

PROTEST: This is a certificate of dishonor provided by a consul, vice consul, notary public, or other person so authorized when an instrument presented for acceptance or payment is refused.

pt.: Port.

R.: Railroad.

RATE OF EXCHANGE: The rate at which the currency of one country is exchanged for the currency of another country.

The central bank rate of exchange is established by a country's central bank. This rate usually is the same as, or close to, the official rate of exchange.

r. & c.c.: Riots and civil commotion.

rcd.: Received.

REBATE RATE: The rate per cent deductible if a bill of exchange or draft is paid before its maturity date.

REMITTING BANK: Bank which sends draft to overseas bank for collection.

R.o.D.: Refused on delivery.

RR: Railroad.

rte.: Route.

s.: Signed.

s.a.: Without year or date.

SAMPLING: The process whereby an inspector will take a portion of a commodity from a larger supply to determine the quality of the total supply for the purpose of grading it for sale to a purchaser.

S.D.B.L.: Sight draft, bill of lading attached.

SIGHT DRAFT: A draft payable upon presentation to the drawee.

S.S.: Steamship.

s. ton: Short ton

STALE DOCUMENT: A document presented after the time customarily allowed for such presentations.

STANDING LETTER OF CREDIT: A letter of credit that is always open.

stg: Sterling.

s.v.: Sailing vessel.

t.:Ton.

TARIFF SCHEDULES: A schedule of duties imposed by a government on imported or, in some countries, exported goods, or a duty or rate of duty imposed in such a schedule.

t.l.: Total loss only.

TON: Freight rates for liner cargo generally are quoted on the basis of a certain rate per ton, depending on the nature of the commodity. This ton, however, may be a weight ton or a measurement ton.

TRADE ACCEPTANCE: A time draft or bill of exchange for the amount of a specific purchase drawn by the seller on the buyer, bearing the buyer's acceptance, and often noting the place of payment.

TRAMP: A tramp ship is a vessel that does not operate along a definite route on a fixed schedule, but calls at any port where cargo is available.

TRUST RECEIPT: This is a document or receipt used in letter of credit financing in which the buyer promises to hold the merchandise received from a bank as trustee for the bank releasing the goods. The effect is that the trustee gets possession of the goods for specified purposes while the bank retains title. Trust receipts are primarily used to permit an importer to hold the merchandise for resale, before paying the issuing bank. The importer is called the trustee, the bank is called the entruster.

USANCE: Period of time between presentation of a draft and its maturity.

U/w: Underwriters.

val: Value.

WAREHOUSE RECEIPT: A receipt supplied by a warehouseman for goods he has placed in storage.

Negotiable: transferable by endorsement and requiring surrender of a receipt to the warehouseman for delivery of the goods.

Non-Negotiable: indicates the nontransferability; goods will be delivered only to the person named therein or to a third party only on written order, i.e., delivery order.

WEIGHT:

Gross: generally, the total weight of the shipped merchandise including all containers and packing material.

Legal: generally, the weight of the merchandise plus the immediate container, a definition that varies somewhat by country.

Net: generally, the weight of the merchandise unpacked, exclusive of containers. This definition also varies somewhat in other countries.

WEIGHT/MEASUREMENT TON: In many cases, a shipping rate is shown “per weight/measurement ton, carriers option.” This means that the rate will be assessed on either a weight ton specified, for example, at 2,240 pounds or measurement ton, at 40 cubic feet, whichever will yield the carrier a greater revenue.

WEIGHT TON: There are three types of weight ton—the short ton, 2000 pounds; the long ton, 2,240 pounds; and the metric ton, 2,204.68 pounds. The metric ton frequently is quoted for cargo exported from Europe.

WHARFAGE: A charge assessed by docks for the handling of incoming or outgoing merchandise.

W/M: Weight or measurement.

w.p.: Weather permitting.

W/R: Warehouse receipt.

W.R.: War risk.

wt.: Weight.

Appendix G

TARIFF SCHEDULE OF THE UNITED STATES

Following is a sample of the Harmonized Tariff Schedule of the United States

715.40 TARIFF SCHEDULES Schedule 7

Part 2—Optical Goods; Scientific and Professional Instruments; Watches, Clocks, and Timing Devices; Photographic Goods; Motion Pictures; Recordings and Recording Media—Continued

Item	Articles	Rates of duty	
		1	2
	Subpart E.—Watches, Clocks, and Timing Apparatus—Con.		
	Apparatus with watch or clock movements or with synchronous motors, for recording the time of day, or for measuring, recording, or otherwise indicating intervals of time:		
715.40	Pigeon timers	$1.08 each + 15.5% ad val. + 6¢ for each jewel, if any.	$4.50 each + 65% ad val. + 25¢ each jewel, if any.
	Other:		
715.45	Valued not over $1.10 each	16.5¢ each + 19% ad val. + 7.5¢ for each jewel, if any.	55¢ each + 65% ad val. + 25¢ each jewel, if any.
715.47	Valued over $1.10 but not over $2.25 each	30¢ each + 19% ad val. + 7.5¢ for each jewel, if any.	$1 each + 65% ad val. + 25¢ each jewel, if any.
715.49	Valued over $2.25 but not over $5 each	45¢ each + 19% ad val. + 7.5¢ for each jewel, if any.	$1.50 each + 65% ad val. + 25¢ each jewel, if any.
715.51	Valued over $5 but not over $10 each	90¢ each + 19% ad val. + 7.5¢ for each jewel, if any.	$3 each + 65% ad val. + 25¢ each jewel, if any
715.53	Valued over $10 each	$1.35 each + 21% ad val. + 7.5¢ for each jewel, if any.	$4.50 each + 65% ad val. + 25¢ each jewel, if any.
	Time switches with watch or clock movements, or with synchronous or subsynchronous motors:		
715.60	Valued not over $1.10 each	16.5¢ each + 19% ad val. + 7.5¢ for each jewel, if any.	55¢ each + 65% ad val. + 25¢ each jewel, if any
715.62	Valued over $1.10 each but not over $2.25 each	30¢ each + 19% ad val. + 7.5¢ for each jewel, if any.	$1 each + 65% ad val. + 25¢ each jewel, if any.
715.64	Valued over $2.25 but not over $5 each	45¢ each + 12% ad val. + 7.5¢ for each jewel, if any.	$1.50 each + 65% ad val. + 25¢ each jewel, if any.
715.66	Valued over $5 but not over $10 each	90¢ each + 12% ad val. + 7.5¢ for each jewel, if any.	$3 each + 65% ad val. + 25¢ each jewel, if any.
715.68	Valued over $10 each	$1.35 each + 19.5% ad val. + 7.5¢ for each jewel, if any.	$4.50 each + 65% ad val. + 25¢ each jewel, if any.

Item	Articles	1-a	1-b	2
	Watch movements, assembled, without dials or hands, or with dials or hands whether or not assembled thereon:[1]			
716.08	Having over 17 jewels	$6.45 each	$10.75 each.	
	Having no jewels or not over 17 jewels:			
	Not adjusted, not self-winding (or if a self-winding device cannot be incorporated therein), and not constructed or designed to operate for a period in excess of 47 hours without rewinding:			
	Having no jewels or only 1 jewel:			
716.10	Not over 0.6 inch in width	90¢ each	$1.50 each	$1.50 each.
716.11	Over 0.6 but not over 0.8 inch in width	75¢ each	$1.35 each	$1.35 each.
716.12	Over 0.8 but not over 0.9 inch in width	75¢ each	$1.20 each	$1.20 each.
716.13	Over 0.9 but not over 1 inch in width	75¢ each	$1.05 each	$1.05 each.
716.14	Over 1 but not over 1.2 inches in width	75¢ each	93¢ each	93¢ each.
716.15	Over 1.2 but not over 1.5 inches in width	75¢ each	84¢ each	84¢ each.
716.16	Over 1.5 but not over 1.77 inches in width	75¢ each	75¢ each	75¢ each.
	Having over 1 jewel but not over 7 jewels:			
716.20	Not over 0.6 inch in width	$1.80 each	$2.50 each	$2.50 each.
716.21	Over 0.6 but not over 0.8 inch in width	$1.35 each	$2.25 each	$2.25 each.
716.22	Over 0.8 but not over 0.9 inch in width	$1.35 each	$2 each	$2 each.
716.23	Over 0.9 but not over 1 inch in width	$1.20 each	$1.75 each	$1.75 each.
716.24	Over 1 but not over 1.2 inches in width	90¢ each	$1.55 each	$1.55 each.
716.25	Over 1.2 but not over 1.5 inches in width	90¢ each	$1.40 each	$1.40 each.
716.26	Over 1.5 but not over 1.77 inches in width	90¢ each	$1.25 each	$1.25 each.
	Having over 7 but not over 17 jewels:			
716.30	Not over 0.6 inch in width	$1.60 each + 9¢ for each jewel over 7.	$2.50 each + 15¢ for each jewel over 7.	
716.31	Over 0.6 but not over 0.8 inch in width	$1.35 each + 9¢ for each jewel over 7.	$2.25 each + 15¢ for each jewel over 7.	
716.32	Over 0.8 but not over 0.9 inch in width	$1.35 each + 9¢ for each jewel over 7.	$2 each + 15¢ for each jewel over 7.	
716.33	Over 0.9 but not over 1 inch in width	$1.20 each + 9¢ for each jewel over 7.	$1.75 each + 15¢ for each jewel over 7.	
716.34	Over 1 but not over 1.2 inches in width	90¢ each + 9¢ for each jewel over 7.	$1.55 each + 15¢ for each jewel over 7.	
716.35	Over 1.2 but not over 1.5 inches in width	90¢ each + 9¢ for each jewel over 7.	$1.40 each + 15¢ for each jewel over 7.	
716.36	Over 1.5 but not over 1.77 inches in width	90¢ each + 9¢ for each jewel over 7.	$1.25 each + 15¢ for each jewel over 7.	
717.00	Adjusted, but not self-winding (and if a self-winding device cannot be incorporated therein), and not constructed or designed to operate for a period in excess of 47 hours without rewinding	Column 1 base rate + 50¢ for each adjustment.	Column 2 base rate + $1 for each adjustment.	
718.00	Self-winding (or if a self-winding device can be incorporated therein), or constructed or designed to operate for a period in excess of 47 hours without rewinding, but not adjusted.	Column 1 base rate + 50¢ each.	Column 2 base rate + $1 each.	
719.00	Adjusted and self-winding (or if a self-winding device can be incorporated therein), or constructed or designed to operate for a period in excess of 47 hours without rewinding.	Column 1 base rate + 50¢ each + 50¢ for each adjustment.	Column 2 base rate + $1 each + $1 for each adjustment.	
	Clock movements, assembled, without dials or hands, or with dials or hands whether or not assembled thereon:			
	Measuring less than 1.77 inches in width:			
	Not constructed or designed to operate for over 47 hours without rewinding:			
20.02	Having no jewels or only 1 jewel	45¢ each	75¢ each.	
20.04	Having over 1 jewel	75¢ each + 8.1¢ for each jewel over 7.	$1.25 each + 15¢ for each jewel over 7.	

Item	Articles	1	2
	Constructed or designed to operate for over 47 hours without rewinding:		
720.06	Having no jewels or only 1 jewel	90¢ each	$1.75 each.
720.08	Having over 1 jewel	$1.20 each + 8.1¢ for each jewel over 7.	$2.25 each + 15¢ for each jewel over 7.
	Other clock movements:		
720.10	Valued not over $1.10 each	16.5¢ each + 19% ad val. + 7.5¢ for each jewel, if any.	55¢ each + 65% ad val. + 25¢ each jewel, if any.
720.12	Valued over $1.10 but not over $2.25 each	30¢ each + 19% ad val. + 7.5¢ for each jewel, if any.	$1 each + 65% ad val. + 25¢ each jewel, if any.
720.14	Valued over $2.25 but not over $5 each	45¢ each + 19% ad val. + 7.5¢ for each jewel, if any.	$1.50 each + 65% ad val. + 25¢ each jewel, if any.

Part 2—Optical Goods; Scientific and Professional Instruments; Watches, Clocks, and Timing Devices; Photographic Goods; Motion Pictures; Recordings and Recording Media—Continued

Item	Articles	Rates of duty	
		1	2
	Subpart E.—Watches, Clocks, and Timing Apparatus—Con.		
	Clock movements, assembled, without dials or hands, or with dials or hands whether or not assembled thereon—Continued		
	Other clock movements—Continued		
720.16	Valued over $5 but not over $10 each	90¢ each + 19% ad val. + 7.5¢ for each jewel, if any.	$3 each + 65% ad val. + 25¢ fo each jewel if any.
720.18	Valued over $10 each	$1.35 each + 19% ad val. + 7.5¢ for each jewel, if any.	$4.50 each + 65% ad val. + 25¢ for each jewel, if any.
	Watch cases and parts thereof:		
	Wholly or almost wholly of gold or platinum or of both gold and platinum:		
720.20	Cases	45¢ each + 18% ad val	75¢ each + 45% ad val.
	Parts:		
720.21	Bezels, backs, and centers	22¢ each + 18% ad val.	75¢ each + 45% ad val.
720.22	Other	24% ad val.	65% ad val.
	Not wholly and not almost wholly of gold or platinum or of both gold and platinum:		
	Wholly or in part of silver; or containing gold or platinum; or set, or prepared to be set, with precious or semiprecious stones or with imitation gemstones:		
720.24	Cases	24¢ each + 18% ad val	40¢ each + 45% ad val.
	Parts:		
720.25	Bezels, backs, and centers	12¢ each + 18% ad val	20¢ each + 45% ad val.
720.26	Other	18% ad val	65% ad val.
	Other:		
720.28	Cases	6¢ each + 12% ad val	20¢ each + 45% ad val.
720.29	Bezels, backs, and centers	3¢ each + 12% ad val	10¢ each + 45% ad val.
720.30	Other	11% ad val.	45% ad val.
	Clock cases, cases for time switches or for other apparatus provided for in this subpart, and parts of the foregoing cases:		
	Clock cases and parts thereof:		
720.32	Over 50 percent of metal by weight and wholly or in part of precious metal.	22% ad val	60% ad val.
	Other:		
720.33	Outer cases for travel clocks	12% ad val	45% ad val.
720.34	Other	16% ad val	45% ad val.
720.36	Other cases and parts	18% ad val	45% ad val.
	Dials and parts thereof:		
	Watch and clock dials:		
720.40	Under 1.77 inches in width	1.5¢ each + 27% ad val	5¢ each + 45% ad val.
720.42	1.77 inches or more in width	15% ad val.	50% ad val.
720.44	Other	30% ad val.	50% ad val.

EXAMPLE OF CALCULATION OF DUTY AT TARIFF RATES AND AT THE NONCOMMERCIAL FLAT RATE

The following is an example appearing in Title 19, Code of Federal Regulations, Section 148.101 (19 CFR 148.101) and in Subsections (b) and (c) of 19 CFR 148.102.

Example: B returned from Europe where he acquired merchandise having a fair retail value of $1,050. Assume for purposes of this example that (1) in addition to the personal exemption of $400, $100 of the merchandise carries a free rate of duty, (2) allowances and exemptions have not been used within the past 30 days, and (3) all articles in excess of allowances and exemptions and duty-free articles are dutiable at rates other than the flat rate.

B presents his baggage to the Customs officer for examination and his declaration for verification. Duty is figured as follows:

FAIR RETAIL VALUE	
(a) The $400 personal exemption	$400
(b) Articles which carry a free rate of duty	$100
(c) The $1,000 flat rate of duty allowance calculated at 10% for the first $1,000	$100
(d) Balance of articles subject to duty at rates other than flat rate	*450 (*)
TOTAL	*1,050 (*)

*The articles not covered by exemptions, allowances, and duty-free rates will be valued under section 402, Tariff Act of 1930, as amended, and duty calculated at rates other than the flat rate.

Insular possessions.

The rate of duty on articles accompanying any person, including a crew member, arriving in the United States directly or indirectly from American Samoa, Guam, or the Virgin Islands of the United States (exclusive of duty-free articles), acquired in these insular possessions as an incident of the person's physical presence there, shall be 5 percent of the fair retail value in the insular possession in which acquired.

Canada. The rate of duty on originating goods from Canada (exclusive of duty-free goods) as defined in § 10.303 of this chapter, accompanying any person, including a crew member, arriving in the United States directly or indirectly from Canada shall be a flat rate of 9 percent as established by the United States-Canada Free-Trade Agreement. The flat rate shall decrease at the rate of one percent every year commencing on January 1, 1990, until January 1, 1998, at which time the free rate of duty shall apply.

IMPORTING IN THE YEARS AHEAD

A book has limitations in providing timely, specific advice to its readers in such a changing field as importing. It must be somewhat general, and the lead time before publication and distribution can be delaying. We feel this book is enough ahead of events to give most of its readers the information they need to make prudent determinations on how to import, and indeed whether to import. However, we know conditions can and often do change rapidly. Consequently we have initiated an advisory newsletter, updating information and giving additional specific and specialized information and advice.

If you think you may be interested in our newsletter, send your name and address to: *Travelers Guide to Importing,* c/o Ten Speed Press, P.O. Box 7123, Berkeley, California 94707. We will also be giving seminars on this subject, and information about them may be obtained at the same address.

Mary Green
Stanley Gillmar

NOTES
MERCHANDISE

NOTES

MERCHANDISE

NOTES
ITINERARY

NOTES
ITINERARY

NOTES
CUSTOMS

NOTES

CUSTOMS